The Complete
Silky Terrier

The Complete
Silky Terrier

Peggy Smith

HOWELL BOOK HOUSE

New York

Collier Macmillan Canada
Toronto

Maxwell Macmillan International
New York   Oxford   Singapore   Sydney

Howell Book House
Macmillan Publishing Company
866 Third Avenue
New York, NY 10022

Collier Macmillan Canada, Inc.
1200 Eglinton Avenue East, Suite 200
Don Mills, Ontario M3C 3N1

Library of Congress Cataloging-in-Publication Data
Smith, Peggy.
    The complete silky terrier/Peggy Smith.
        p.   cm.
    ISBN 0-87605-335-5
    1. Silky terriers. I. Title.
SF429.S66S59   1990
636.7'55—dc20   90-33199

Macmillan books are available at special discounts for bulk purchases for sales promotions, premiums, fund-raising, or educational use. For details contact:

Special Sales Director
Macmillan Publishing Company
866 Third Avenue
New York, NY 10022

10 9 8 7 6 5 4 3 2 1

Printed in the United States of America

Contents

Acknowledgments   vii

1   Origin and History of the Silky Terrier   1

2   The Silky Terrier Comes to America   17

3   The Modern Silky Terrier in America   35

4   The Silky Terrier Around the World   59

5   The Silky Terrier Standards   83

6   Discussion of the Silky Terrier Standard   95

7   Comparison of the Silky, Yorkshire and Australian Terrier Breeds   109

8   The Character of the Silky Terrier   113

9   Choosing a Silky Terrier Puppy   117

10   Caring for a Silky Terrier   123

11   Grooming the Silky Terrier   129

12   Showing the Silky Terrier   141

13 The Winners' Circle   151

14 The Silky Terrier in Obedience and Tracking   169

15 Register of Merit   181

16 The Silky Terrier Clubs   215

    Appendix: Competing in American Kennel Club Shows   221

Acknowledgments

THE AUTHOR wishes to thank everyone who contributed pictures for this book—many are irreplaceable—and especially Mary T. Estrin for her sketches illustrating Silky rights and wrongs. Particular thanks must be given to Silky Terrier fanciers Eleanor Franceschi, Connie Alber, Linda Ann Schulte, Linda Louise Schulte, Florence Males and Laurie Ericson. Their expertise in obedience training, show ring handling and grooming made major contributions to these chapters. The voluminous correspondence from Silky Terrier owners in other countries is also greatly appreciated.

Special thanks are due to my friend Jerry Macfarlane, Pekingese exhibitor, and my husband, Merle, for their interest and the countless hours they spent reading the drafts of the manuscript, as well as for their invaluable questions and suggestions.

The Complete
Silky Terrier

Ch. Redway Wexford Peter's Poppy, pictured at sixteen years of age in 1989. By Ch. Redway For Pete's Sake out of Ch. Redway Black Eyed Susan, CD, bred by Eleanor Franceschi and Peggy Smith, owned by Peggy Smith. Poppy is a granddaughter of Ch. Wexford Pogo, who was born in 1952! *Margaret Coder*

1

Origin and History
of the Silky Terrier

$\mathbf{M}$ANY OPINIONS have been written concerning the origin of the Silky Terrier—almost as many as the assortment of names the breed has been called: Australian Terrier (silky coated), Sydney Silky Terrier, Victorian Silky Terrier, Soft and Silky Terrier, and Silky Toy Terrier. In their native Australia they have been officially called Australian Silky Terriers since 1956.

One fact agreed upon by all breed historians is that they emerged as a "by-product" during the establishment of the Australian Terrier. Therefore, a study of the history of the Australian Terrier is essential to the history of the Silky Terrier.

No records were kept of exactly which terrier breeds were used in creating the Australian Terrier. Writers who have speculated on the breed's origin have mentioned Skye Terriers, Dandie Dinmont Terriers, Manchester Terriers, Norwich Terriers, Border Terriers, red or sandy Cairn Terriers and the now extinct Clydesdale or Paisley Terriers.

The earliest available history of the Australian Terrier is contained in *The Dog In Australasia,* by Walter Beilby, published in

Australia in 1897. It is a voluminous book of almost five hundred pages devoted to more than fifty breeds of dogs, including some which had not yet arrived in Australia and others that were already extinct. Included are full-page photographs, etchings or copies of paintings of nearly every breed mentioned, as well as numerous pedigrees.

Mr. Beilby dedicated the book to "My Esteemed Friend, Frederick W. Haddon, Of South Yarra, Melbourne, Victoria, President Of The Victorian Poultry And Kennel Club, As A Grateful Acknowledgment Of The Great Services He Has Rendered To Australian Breeders And Exhibitors Of High-Class Stock By His Good Example And Influence; Also For The Valuable Assistance He Has Given To Me In The Production Of This Book, The First Of The Kind Ever Published In The Australasian Colonies."

His preface reads, in part:

It was with great reluctance and diffidence that I yielded to the persuasive powers of the publishers of this book, and undertook the responsibility of attempting to supply a work on the Dog in Australasia, which, while containing information useful to colonial fanciers generally, should be so written as to be of special service to beginners.

As my readers will observe, I have not attempted to carry my researches back to remote antiquity, contenting myself with a brief history of each breed from the time when systematic, or at any rate, record breeding was first commenced.

One of the greatest difficulties that faces the young breeder in these colonies is the absence of a published "Stud Book." The consequence is that very little information can be obtained by the great majority of breeders as to the early importations of dogs—indeed, any knowledge of the progenitors of their stock further than a few generations back. This is a great drawback, that must be apparent to the merest tyro.

In the absence of a registered breeding table [*author's note:* referred to previously as "Stud Book"], unprincipled breeders and dealers have been enabled for years past to carry on their nefarious practices unchecked, and thus an immense amount of damage has been done to the canine fancy in Australasia.

Fortunately, a good start on the road of reform has been made by the leading societies and clubs, within the last few years, by the adoption of the English principle of only allowing registered dogs to be entered at shows, and by not permitting the duplication of names.

I fully recognize that I cannot in this work give a complete record

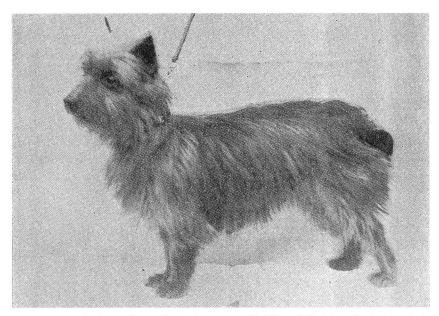

The illustration of a Rough-Coated Terrier that appeared in Walter Beilby's *The Dog in Australasia,* published in Australia in 1897.

W. G. Borron's Wolden Scottish Wonder, a Scottish Terrier, an illustration of the breed in Australia that appeared in *The Dog in Australasia* in 1897. It's highly probable that the Scottish Terrier was used in the formation of the Australian Terrier.

Australian ⌇ Terrier.

The Australian Terrier

"SANDOW"

At Stud.

ʜᴇ is a rich blue and tan in colour, and is a very t⟨ terrier. He has won at all the leading shows in Victoria— in fact, neither he or his mother (Wᴀᴛᴛʟᴇ) have been beaten yet.

STUD FEE, £1 10s.

ALSO, "JACK,"

A younger dog, full brother to Sandow.

He is a good blue and tan, very low set, and a sure stock-getter.

FEE, £1.

Pups always on hand.

For further particulars apply

SAMS & STOBIE,
67 Buckingham Street,
SYDNEY, N.SW.

An advertisement for Sandow, an Australian Terrier, in *The Dog in Australasia*.

of all the early importations, nor can I furnish the pedigrees so fully as I should like to do, but in the pedigree tables supplied, and in the comments on the various breeds, the ancestry of most of the leading dogs imported into the Australian colonies since 1880 will be found traceable. This in itself, I trust, will make the book acceptable to many besides beginners.

The short history of the growth of the fancy in these colonies, with a reference to some of the earlier attempts at dog shows, may perhaps be read with interest.

The terrier breeds featured in the book were the Airedale Terrier, Black and Tan or Manchester Terrier, Rough or Broken-haired Terrier, Bull Terrier, Clydesdale or Paisley Terrier, Dandie Dinmont Terrier, Smooth Fox Terrier, Rough or Wirehaired Fox Terrier, Irish Terrier, Skye Terrier, Scottish Terrier, Welsh Terrier, White English Terrier and the only toy, the Yorkshire Terrier. Of these breeds, the following had already reached Australia: Airedale, Black and Tan or Manchester, Bull, Dandie Dinmont, Smooth Fox, Rough or Wirehaired Fox, Irish, Skye, Scottish and Yorkshire.

The breed called the Rough or Broken-haired Terrier is regarded as the foundation stock for the Australian Terrier. The first Australian Rough-coated Terrier Club was formed in Victoria in 1889 and held its first show in 1890. The following is Mr. Beilby's description of this breed:

> This is a small dog generally exhibited in classes provided as "other varieties," rough-coated terriers, and classified as blue and tans and sandies. They were, until the latter end of the eighties, known in these colonies as Scotch terriers. In 1889 a club was instituted, known as the Australian Rough-coated Terrier Club, and a standard was drawn up. A couple of small shows were held by the club in the Fitzroy Town Hall, near Melbourne. The committee of this organization applied to the Victorian Poultry and Dog Society (now known under the new title of Victorian Poultry and Kennel Club) to accept the standard and acknowledge, or rather grant, the prefix "Australian," which was most properly refused. As one who has very carefully watched this little animal ever since it was first shown, I am in a position to write from my own personal observation, and I have not the slightest hesitation in pronouncing these dogs arrant nondescripts.
>
> If in the object sought any advantage was to be gained, such as an improvement upon any of the recognized breeds for special work, the movement would have had my sympathy, but they cannot be compared with the Yorkshire for appearance or with the Scottish terrier as a terrier-like dog for use. I mention these two breeds because they

AUSTRALIAN TERRIER.
CHAMPION BLUE CLIPPER (Two Blues—The Colours.)
Winner of 20 Challenge Certificates.
Bred by J. B. Matterson.

SYDNEY SILKY TERRIER.
CHAMPION IDEAL (Sandow—Midget.)
The dog whom the standard was framed from.
Property of J. B. Matterson.

An Australian Terrier and a Sydney Silky Terrier (circa 1906). This Silky, Ch. Ideal, was sired by Sandow, the Australian Terrier. Ideal was the challenge dog winner as a Soft and Silky Terrier at the Sydney (New South Wales) Royal Show, in 1904 and 1905.

are nearest in resemblance to the animals under notice. These little dogs are of all sizes, colours, and shapes—long bodies, short bodies, tall, low set, hard coats, soft coats, and colours that would puzzle a first-class artist to define. In fact, I have never seen a family likeness in any litter, and that they are not indigenous goes without saying. It is quite certain that the dingo has nothing whatever to do with them, and I am not going into the question of this animal's ancestry.

I know that a prominent prize-winner, a champion of his breed, Burr Pincher to wit, a dog whose name was prominently mentioned when the standard was under discussion, was actually advertised at stud as a Scottish terrier. I have in my possession a stud card with this very dog illustrated on it, and a copy of this can be seen in the Victorian Poultry and Dog Society's catalogue of 1887. The matter on the card, however, is more complete, giving amongst other particulars the information that he won a second prize at the Crystal Palace, the date of the show, of course, being carefully omitted.

If Pincher had won a prize at the Crystal Palace as a Scottish terrier he certainly had no right to be considered a champion as a would-be Australian terrier. Besides, if he had won a prize at any of the English Kennel Club shows, he would have had a Kennel Club Stud Book number attached to his name, even if his parentage was obscure, as it appears to be, by the absence of both parents in the Australasian catalogues. His importer's name should also have appeared in the Stock Department's register; all these important details, however, are missing, yet his name appears in gold type with the affix imported, preceded by the words Scotch terrier. His name is also recorded as the sire of winners at one of the special shows referred to, besides others. Another animal that won first and special at the 1888 show of the Victorian Poultry and Dog Society appears as by Duke (imported). Now this bitch is also the dam of a number of winners in these nondescript classes, and yet we find some people still grumbling because the up-to-date canine legislators will not pass a bill granting the name Australian terrier.

Previous to Pincher's time several of these dogs were to be found winning with the affix "Imported," even after the name "Australian" had been applied for. I lent one of the appointed judges the Scottish Terrier Club's standard, and an illustration of the celebrated Champion Dundee, to guide him in his awards to the would-be Australian terrier. This was prior to the advent of the Scottish Terrier at Australian shows. Yet it clearly proved that there was, at any rate, one breeder who recognized that a terrier-like dog was required, and wished to get as near to such as possible. But now we have the genuine article nondescripts are not wanted.

In July last year I was consulted by a Sydney breeder who had an idea that an Irish terrier cross would greatly improve his strain. My advice was to take up the Irish-men and let the cross go. In June this year (1897) I met one of the breeders and exhibitors of this extraordinary variety, and he had with him quite a curiosity in dog-flesh—a low-set, long-backed, long-headed, crooked-legged, badger-coloured creature, of whose parentage he was quite ignorant. Nevertheless, he expressed his belief that the animal would greatly improve his stock. I candidly admitted that I did not think it could do any harm.

About the middle of 1889 a very heated controversy about these dogs took place in the kennel columns of the *Australasian* and the *Leader* [*author's note:* These were newspapers]. The ball was really set rolling in the previous year by Mr. A. Holcroft (of Bedlington fame), who was not far from the pen that used to sign "Scotch Terrier". The letters that appeared under this *nom de plume* were very biting indeed. In one of them the writer referred to the rough terrier as an unmitigated mongrel, and only fit to use where snakes were too numerous to risk a dog of any value. The writer went on to say that they were what would be called in Scotland "Tinkers' Messen" and he finished up by remarking that "we must be thankful that the Victorian Poultry and Dog Society has not allowed the name Australian to be prostituted to such vile uses and hung round the neck of a wretched mongrel. If whimsical or faddish people want an Australian breed, let them take up the dingo and try what they can make of improving him."

What they will be like now cropping is abolished will be quite interesting to watch. One thing is very certain, that the ear carriage, no matter how it varies, will be quite in keeping with the remaining portion of the dog.

The illustration is that of a first prize winner. It conveys a fair idea of the animal under notice, and will probably be interesting to any breeders of "Brussels Griffons" who may happen to obtain a copy of this book.

Mr. Beilby's illustration of the Rough-coated Terrier, pictured in this chapter, more closely resembles a respectable Silky Terrier than a Brussels Griffon of that period or now. *Toy Dogs: How to Breed and Rear Them,* by Muriel Handley Spicer, published in England in 1902, pictures the Brussels Griffon looking as it does today—without the length of muzzle of Mr. Beilby's Rough-coated Terrier illustration. The Brussels Griffon breed was not featured in Mr. Beilby's book, so we can only guess as to whether he was being facetious in this comparison.

Those who were determined to establish a native Australian terrier continued undaunted by the published opinions of Mr. Beilby, Mr. Holcroft and Mr. Coupe.

A litter sired by Ch. Sparkling Armley, circa 1930, identified as Silky Terriers.

An illustration of the extinct Clydesdale, also called the Paisley Terrier, which was a blue and tan dog with a straight silky coat. As measured against the lady's fan in the picture, the breed appears to have been smaller than the Skye Terrier, to which it was related. The Clydesdale Terrier was believed by some to have been used in the formation of the Silky Terrier.

There is no doubt that the Australian Terrier resulted from stock produced by many types of short-legged terriers from Great Britain. Perhaps even the "Yankee" dog that was imported into Australia was one of the progenitors.

Mr. J. C. Coupe, at that time writing under the *nom de plume* "Kennelman," in the *Australasian,* was very caustic in his comments on this class of dog. At the Australian Terrier Club's first show in 1889, he said:—"Many of the visitors doubtless were attracted by a desire to see what class of dog the so-called Australian terrier is. If multiplicity of type is a recommendation they were certainly not disappointed, every imaginable cross, as far as terriers are concerned being amongst the exhibits. To venture to criticise them would be attempting to describe the indescribable."

Other fanciers have informed me of similar dogs being common in Liverpool. A short time ago a dog arrived here from America and was quarantined in Collingwood. This Yankee production was described to me by Mr. R. Harkness (and he certainly ought to know, if anyone does, what breeders have been trying to produce) as a very good sample of this so-called Australian.

I understand that the standard as adopted by the now defunct club has been accepted by one of the dog societies in New South Wales, and that a recent aspirant to fame in canine judgeship was requested to be guided by the lines laid down. To the utter consternation of the exhibitors he said he could disqualify the lot, as not one had a pink nose. This I may mention, was in the list of disqualifications, which the judicial novice had mistaken for an important characteristic of the breed!

Breeders introduced the Yorkshire Terrier in an attempt to improve color in the blue and tan dogs. This resulted in litters in which some dogs resembled the Yorkshire, some resembled the Australian and others had qualities from both breeds. These latter dogs were the forerunners of the Silky Terrier. Breeders were faced with another challenge: to breed a silky-coated, blue and tan dog that was larger and had less coat than the Yorkshire Terrier.

Tyack's Annual, published in the early 1900s, carried a poem attributed to "Turner":

Its sire was Australian, component parts were many,
Yorkshire, Black and Tan and Scotch—it proved much worse
*   than any,*
Another dash of Yorkshire, result was far from pretty,
They called it "Sydney" Silky but quarrel o'er the city.

Ch. Sparkling Armley, a Silky Terrier, circa 1930, when cross-breeding was still permitted. He was bred in the state of Victoria and was a state champion. No record of his sire and dam is available.

Poetic license was used, since Melbourne, the capital of the state of Victoria, was never included in the various names of the breed.

An advertisement for stud service by Sandow, an Australian Terrier, appeared in Mr. Beilby's book. Also pictured is Ch. Ideal, a Sydney Silky Terrier—"the dog whom the standard was framed from." Sandow, an Australian Terrier, was Ideal's sire. Ideal was the challenge dog at the 1904 and 1905 Sydney Royal show in a class called Terrier, Soft and Silky. In 1907 the classification at the Royal was changed to Terrier, Sydney Silky.

In 1908 the Sydney Silky and Yorkshire Terrier Club was organized in the state of New South Wales. Its booklet of rules and regulations contained the following among the objects of the club:

> Stud Book and Produce Register—That the Club shall keep a Stud Book of Sydney Silky Terriers and Yorkshire Terriers, in which every Member of the Club shall have the privilege of registering, free of charge, any stud dog or brood bitch upon the production of a properly verified pedigree. That every Member shall endeavour to promote the correctness of such register by contributing any information respecting the breed that he may possess or acquire. That the Club shall also keep a register of the produce of Sydney Silky and Yorkshire Terriers of verified pedigrees, in which Members of the Club may, without charge, register the particulars of any litters bred by them, and that these books be also opened to non-members on payment to the funds of the Club of a fee of one shilling for each entry or reference.

The first Standard for the breed was adopted and issued by this club in 1906. It read:

SYDNEY SILKY TERRIER

General Appearance of Dog. Rather low-set, compact, active, with good straight (silky) hair.

Head. Head of moderate length, strong, and of terrier character; teeth, level; nose, black; eyes, small and keen and of a dark colour (long hair on head and face objectionable).

Ears. Ears, small, set high on skull; V shaped, falling to front or pricked, clean ears preferred [*author's note:* Meaning free of long hair].

Neck. Neck inclined to be long and strong.

Body. Body rather long in proportion to height, well ribbed up; back straight, and tail docked.

Legs. Forelegs straight, well set under the body. Hindlegs, strong thighs, hocks slightly bent.

Feet. Feet, well padded, cat-like; black or dark toe-nails preferable.

Coat. Coat must be of silky texture; length not less than six inches desirable.

Colour. Colour, blue and tan, or silver-blue and tan; tan markings on muzzle and legs, the richer the better.

Weight. Maximum 12 pounds; minimum 6 pounds.

Defects. White toe-nails, short coat.

Disqualifications. Flesh-colour nose; curly, wavy or woolly coat, mouth much overshot or undershot, under or over weight.

Scale of Points

Coat	20
Colour	15
Head	15
Mouth	10
Body and General Appearance	15
Toe-nails	5
Legs and Feet	10
Ears	5
Eyes	5
Total	100

In 1908, in the state of Victoria, the Victorian Silky and Yorkshire Terrier Club adopted and issued a different Standard. This Standard called for a neck of medium length, the body to be of rather moderate length in proportion to height, and made a wavy coat a defect instead of a disqualification. Two weight classes were noted: one under six pounds, another six pounds and under twelve pounds. Overweight was a disqualification.

During the establishment of the Australian and Silky Terrier breeds, breeders were permitted to register individual pups from litters as whichever breed they most resembled. In 1932 legislation was introduced prohibiting any further cross-breeding. A pure four-generation pedigree was required for kennel club registration.

Until 1959 each Australian state had a slightly different Standard for the breed. That year, with the formation of the Australian National Kennel Council, the first national canine organization, a single Standard was adopted for Silky Terriers, and all breeds be-

A son of Ch. Sparkling Armley, circa 1930, identified as a Silky Terrier.

Strathdene Silky Boy, a Silky Terrier, son of Ch. Sparkling Armley, circa 1930. His littermate, Strathdene Sad Kelly, was registered as an Australian Terrier.

came eligible to compete for the title of Australian champion. Prior to this the championship titles were limited to the state in which they had completed the requirements.

We should be thankful that the early breeders of Australian Terriers and Silky Terriers refused to be discouraged by their critics. They would be proud to see the results of their efforts.

A 1940 photograph of Jack and Jill, owned by Mrs. George Walker of Manhasset, New York.

2

The Silky Terrier Comes to America

T HE FIRST Silky Terriers known to have come to America were two Australian imports in the early 1930s. They were pictured in the February 1936 issue of the *National Geographic Magazine,* identified as Smart Tone, "long haired and silvery gray," and Dream Girl, "shorter haired and colored black and tan with just a little gray." Smart Tone was registered in Australia as Beaconsfield Smart Tone (by Aus. Ch. Sir Rex out of Beaconsfield Jess). He was born in 1933. Dream Girl's breeding is unknown. They were imported by Mrs. G. E. Thomas of Washington, D.C.

Mrs. George Walker, of Manhasset, New York, owned one of their get for fifteen years. She also owned another pair of Silky Terriers, Jack and Jill, whose breeding is unknown.

There are no known present-day descendants of any of these early imports.

A few other Silky Terriers were imported from Australia to California in the late 1940s, but only Roland and Betty Stegeman's Donny Brook Topsy (by Daniel out of Nellie) can be traced to current-day Silky Terriers.

Other 1940s imports found in the pedigrees of present-day Silky Terriers were those of Geoffrey and Martha Sutcliffe of Charlotte, North Carolina. Geoffrey was a prisoner of war in Shanghai during World War II, and Martha became intrigued with the breed while living in Australia awaiting his release. After their return to the United States, the Sutcliffes imported two dogs and a bitch from Australia. The dogs were Kelso Dinkum (by Tharlab Teddy out of Miss Judy of Deandale) and Wee Waa Aussie (by Wee Jacky out of Peggy). The bitch was Glenbrae Sally (by Blamey Boy of Deandale out of Diana of Deandale). All were born in 1948.

The Sutcliffes established the first Silky Terrier kennel in the United States and bred a number of litters until the early 1970s. Their line comes down to present-day Silky Terriers, primarily through Kanimbla Lady Penelope (by Kanimbla Sir Potch out of Kanimbla Fatima). She was the first Silky Terrier owned by Nettie Simmons of Newport, Rhode Island, the first Silky breeder in that area. She was the breeder of Ch. Clavons Blue Rain (by Ch. Redway Beau Brummell out of Kanimbla Lady Penelope). Blue Rain sired seventeen champions and was owned by Betty Young.

In 1951 Peggy and Merle Smith imported a bitch puppy from Australia to California as Peggy's Christmas present. This was Brenhill Splinters (by Prishwood Sir Teddy out of Ellwyn Lady Judy). In 1952 they imported a five-month-old male, Wexford Pogo (by Baulkham Royal John out of Elouera Joy). Both were bought as pets but were well chosen for breeding by Mrs. M. J. Brennan, whose kennel prefix was Brenhill. Their mutual grandsire was Aus. Ch. Ellwyn Gold Prince, who was described as "one of the best in his show days" by Ivy Milne of the Australian Aldoon prefix.

In 1954 Merle, a pilot for Pan American Airways, was transferred to New York. While living there Pogo and Splinters produced a litter, and the Smiths began showing in the Miscellaneous class at American Kennel Club (AKC) shows. It was at the 1954 Westchester Kennel Club show that the well-known animal photographer, Walter Chandoha, "discovered" the breed. Wexford Pogo was entered at this show, and his puppy, Redway Blue Boy, was brought along to keep him company. This outgoing young pup captivated Mr. Chandoha.

He writes of this encounter in his book, *Walter Chandoha's Book of Puppies and Dogs,* published by Crown Publishers in 1969:

A good example of a dog's happy personality being reflected in his photographs is that of a Silky Terrier I met some time ago at a dog

Brenhill Splinters.

Aus. Ch. Kelso Lady Susan.

show. . . . I came upon a Silky Terrier watching all the activity. He was completely at ease and unperturbed by the hubbub around him. As I bent down to pet him, his tail wagged furiously and his bright eyes said hello. If the dog was this friendly, happy, and alert in all the confusion of the dog show, I figured he'd be even more so in the quiet of my studio. So I waited for his owner to appear. She was a most attractive young lady.

I identified myself and asked if we might arrange a mutually convenient time for her to come to my studio with the dog for a photographic session. As I handed her my card, it occurred to me that everything I said sounded like the old come-up-and-see-my-etchings proposition. To allay any suspicion along these lines, I made sure to mention that my wife would probably answer the phone when she called to arrange a shooting date. She called the following week, and the photographs we made of her charming dog were everything I had expected.

Rarely do I ask an owner to bring a dog to my studio to be photographed unless I have a specific assignment, but when I find a model as appealing as that little Silky Terrier, I make every effort to fit him into my shooting schedule. The pictures that resulted turned out to be very successful.

Shortly after this the Smiths were transferred to Miami. They received a letter from Walter Chandoha saying that a picture of Redway Blue Boy would appear on the cover of the November 28, 1954, issue of *This Week Magazine,* a nationally syndicated Sunday newspaper supplement. This cover picture is reproduced in this book.

The sidelines in the magazine read:

The Cover: We doubt very much if you can identify the breed of the raffish little dog on our cover, so we're going to tell you right off to save you the trouble. He's a Sydney Silky Terrier named Redway Blue Boy, or simply Reddy to his owner, Mrs. Margaret Smith of Miami, Florida. The Sydney Silky Terrier is a rare breed in the United States, where, we're told, there are only about 30 of them. They're distantly related to the Yorkshire Terrier, and their principal barking grounds are (as you may have guessed) in Australia, where they are very popular.

The Sydney Silky Terrier is not listed by the American Kennel Club. However, the few who own them hope that their popularity and numbers will increase to the point that AKC will offer them official registration.

The *This Week Magazine* cover picture created a sensation nationwide! Although no address was given for "Margaret Smith of

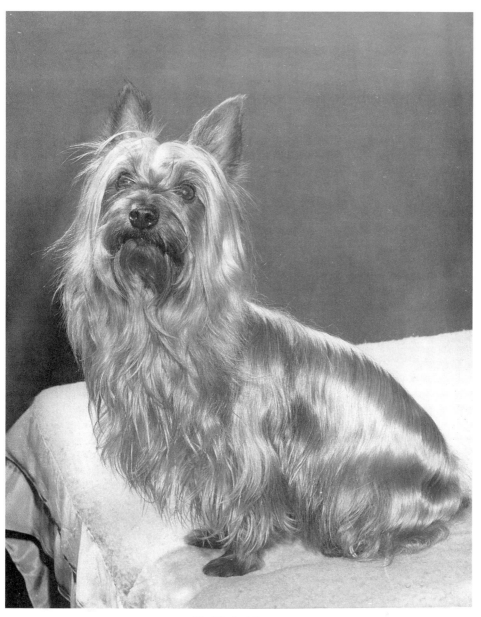

Ch. Wexford Pogo.

Miami, Florida," mail was delivered with just that address thanks to the diligence of the telephone company, the postal service, and even the Bureau of Missing Persons! She received more than 300 letters within the next month. Breeders in Australia were inundated with inquiries, since there were only a handful of breeders in the United States, and within the next year more than one hundred Silky Terrier puppies were imported.

This Week Magazine published a sequel to the cover picture in their April 3, 1955, issue. The article was titled "Rush One Puppy," and pictured a Silky puppy and his new owner holding a copy of the November cover picture. The subtitle was "A Little Dog from Down Under Traveled 8000 Miles to a New Home," and the story read:

> Last November we printed a picture of a Sydney Silky Terrier on our cover. Some 200 readers wrote us asking how to get one of these dogs—and one enterprising lady got in touch with Australia. Mrs. Evelyn Holaday, of La Crescenta, California, asked Qantas Empire Airways to ship her a Sydney Silky—and they did. A six week old pup named Sir Boomerang made the 8000 mile trip. Said one official: "Thank heavens *This Week Magazine* didn't publish a photograph of a kangaroo." The airline doesn't intend to make a practice of this service.

"Never-Ending" was the title of a follow-up article in the Sidelines column of the June 5, 1955, issue of *This Week Magazine.* It read:

> A lot of things have happened since Redway Blue Boy, pictured below, appeared on our cover last November 28. The perky little Sydney Silky Terrier, a rare breed in this country, captivated our pet-loving readers with the following results: A California lady ordered a six week old Silky direct from Australia. She named it Sir Boomerang. Hugh E. Paine, President of the American Society for the Prevention of Cruelty to Animals, imported two dogs to New York on the basis of the cover picture. He had never seen a Silky before.
>
> Most important to Silky fans, our cover picture spurred the founding of the Sydney Silky Terrier Club of America. So far, according to the organization's Corresponding Secretary, Howard A. Jensen, more than 50 owners with about 75 Silky Terriers have been located in eight states.

Interest in the breed in America had reached such proportions that, on October 30, 1955, the Australian News and Information Bureau issued a news release titled "Australia's Silky Terrier a Rival for Koala Bear," bylined by Frances Minahan. It read, in part:

REDDY: HE'S ONE OF 30 IN THE U.S. SEE SIDELINES, PAGE 2

Redway Blue Boy in the picture that popularized Silky Terriers in the United States. He was a son of Peggy Smith's Australian imports, Wexford Pogo and Brenhill Splinters.   *Walter Chandoha*

23

The Australian Silky Terrier, which is the name of the cute little fellow pictured on this page, looks like it is becoming a potential rival for Australia's famous Koala Bear in overseas popularity.

Also a denizen of "Down Under" the small dog has a wide appeal to Australian dog fanciers who are pleased to learn of his growing popularity in the United States.

Since the arrival in the United States this year of Sir Boomerang, the Australian Silky Terrier owned by Mrs. Evelyn Holaday of La Crescenta, California, who became a nationwide canine ambassador for Australia in the United States, a number of the little Australians have left Australia to make their home in the United States.

When Ann Miller, the Hollywood star, arrived in Australia on tour this year she was asked what souvenir she would like to take back to America from Australia.

She replied: "I would love to have one of those little Silky Terriers." So she is now a proud owner of an Australian Silky Terrier.

Latest emigrant is the appealing little three months old Silky pictured on this page who is leaving Sydney to go to its new owner, Mr. Robert Cooley of Northridge, California. This puppy, Aldoon Bonnie, is a daughter of Champion Aldoon Prince, Australian Silky Terrier, who was a Reserve Challenge Winner in the Australian Silky Award at Sydney's Royal Agricultural Show. He is owned by Mrs. Milne of Randwick, Sydney.

At most dog shows throughout Australia the Australian Silky Terrier (or as he is known in the United States, the Sydney Silky) is among the prize winners.

He is bred in all six States of Australia and in New South Wales alone there are two hundred registered breeders. This no doubt accounts for the change in his name at an Interstate Conference held in April 1954 from the "Sydney Silky Terrier" to the "Australian Silky Terrier." Breeders in other States probably did not want to see Sydney alone having the "title" to the little fellow. In the United States, however, the small dog is still known as the Sydney Silky.

First bred in Sydney, he is the result of cross-breeding between the Yorkshire and the Australian Terrier. Breed history really began in the 1890s when fanciers of the small terriers of those days—the Skye and Yorkshire—experienced difficulty in retaining correct body colour under Australian summer conditions. Colour faded rapidly in the sun and demand for puppies fell off, particularly from new arrivals to Australia, who were accustomed to much darker dogs.

Dandie Dinmont, Black and Tan and Irish Terriers were crossed by various breeders, who found that the dogs bred fairly true to type, except in regard to coat texture.

Enthusiasts of these new types got together in 1898 to form the "Australian Terrier Club" and decided that two coats would be recognized—the Australian Terrier (rough coated) and the Australian Terrier (silky coated).

As time went by the rough coated variety became more rugged in type while the silky coated dog threw back to his original ancestor, the Yorkshire Terrier, as breeders concentrated on breeding for coat texture.

Some ten years later the Silky became known as the Sydney Silky Terrier in New South Wales but retained Silky Terrier for his official name in the State of Victoria.

Standards prescribed by the governing body in New South Wales, the Royal Agriculture Society Kennel Club, are a height of approximately ten inches and weight of between six and 12 pounds. The dog's coat should be fine and glossy and of a silky texture; not less than six inches desirable.

Before the breed is officially recognized by the American Kennel Club it must be registered as a pure bred dog by the United States Department of Agriculture, Washington, D.C. Captain Will Judy, chairman of the "National Dog Week" committee, who has been in Australia from the United States to judge dogs at the 1955 Royal Agriculture Show in Melbourne, Victoria, stated that he intends making representation on behalf of this breed when he returns to the United States.

Another picture of Redway Blue Boy appeared on the cover of the December 1955 *Popular Photography* magazine. This photograph kindled the interest of Beverly and Bill Lehnig, of Louisville, Kentucky. Using the Rebel prefix, they became the first Silky breeders in the Midwest, beginning with D'Under Count Chequers (by Redway Lord Teasel out of Sangate Lady Crumpets) and the imported Aldoon Countess Candy (by Glenboig Tim out of Aldoon Lassie).

On September 23, 1956, another nationally syndicated Sunday newspaper supplement, *Family Weekly Magazine,* featured the now famous pup on the cover. This and the *Popular Photography* cover picture resulted in more imports from Australia and a few from New Zealand.

Sports Illustrated magazine featured a two-page spread on Silky Terriers in their April 7, 1958, issue. Pictured were Wexford Pogo and a litter of pups bred by Robert Cooley. John Bryson was the photographer. The picture was taken in September 1955 at Mr. Cooley's home in southern California, where a group of fanciers, including some from northern California, gathered for an evaluation of their dogs by Australian all-breed judge Fred David.

Publicity in local newspapers also played a large part in popularizing the breed. The *San Francisco Examiner,* on June 19, 1955, featured Tom Fromm's Sangate Earl Jocko (by Redway Splinters' Boy out of Greenhills Lady Moppet), along with a lengthy article about the breed's quest for recognition. The *San Francisco Chronicle* pictured two unidentified Silky Terriers, owned by Margaret Citrino, in their August 14, 1955, edition and noted, "Rarely does a breed new to this country take the public's fancy as completely and quickly as has the Silky."

"A Vanderbilt Goes to the Dogs" was the title of an article in the *New York Mirror* magazine on June 23, 1957. It pictured Mrs. Consuelo Vanderbilt Earl's Australian import, Veda Iradell Megsy (by Aus. Ch. Milan Blue Bandit out of Veda Franzi). Mrs. Earl had been mentioned in the "Chic-Chat" column of the March 13, 1957, New York *Daily News,* which read: "Mrs. N. Clarkson Earl, the former Consuelo Vanderbilt, just back from a Far East cruise, has brought nine Australian Silky Terriers to add to her collection of unusual animals at her farm in Ridgefield, Connecticut. There, Consie has miniature horses and cows with sheds, kennels, cages and perches filled with odd critters."

The state of Montana entered the scene in 1957 with two feature articles. The June 26 edition of the *Great Falls Tribune* pictured Mrs. Carl Suhr and her Redway Sir Smidgen (by Wexford Pogo out of Brenhill Splinters); on September 12 the *Great Falls Leader* pictured Smidge and the newly arrived D'Under Miss La Petite (by Aldoon Clipper out of Waratah Winsome Winner), owned by Doradene Robison.

Philadelphia's *Sunday Bulletin* of September 8, 1957, announced the coming sixth annual Rittenhouse Square Dog Show in observance of National Dog Week and pictured Redway Beau Brummell (by Wexford Pogo out of Brenhill Splinters), owned by Suzanne Richardson and Phyllis Buchanan. The Rittenhouse Square Dog Show continued until the early 1970s. The individual breed representatives were there "by invitation." The show was held in downtown Philadelphia and, as described in the article:

> The canine pageant will embrace all facets of purebred dogdom, opening with a pack demonstration by the oldest organized hunt in America. The Rose Tree Hunt, of Media, Pennsylvania, will move into Rittenhouse Square with several couple of American Foxhounds, accompanied by their liveried Master of Foxhounds, Huntsman, and Whipper-In. The Square is an appropriate setting for America's most distinguished hunt, whose Foxhounds trace their ancestry back to

Koolamina Aussie, one of the early breed champions, was an Australian import, born in 1955 (by Prairie Possom out of Aus. Ch. Kendoral Sybil). Bred by H. W. Patterson, he was imported and owned by Lucille Tindall Preston, one of the most industrious of the breed pioneers. She was one of the founders of the Silky Terrier Club of Southern California, which later became the City of Angels Silky Terrier Club.

Aus. Ch. Bowenvale Murray.

those which led the field in which George Washington "rode to hounds."

The format of other years will be observed. The six groups of pedigreed dogdom will alternate with a field trial demonstration, obedience drills and trained dog acts. Again, each group will be reviewed by a star of radio and television who will select "the dog I'd like most to take home with me." This time, however, the judges will be men of fame, instead of women as in former years.

. . . The purpose of these demonstrations, in fact, of the whole show, is to get across to the public the versatility, intelligence, variety and beauty of purebred dogdom.

The *Newark Sunday News* carried a two-page spread on September 8, 1957, featuring rare breeds and picturing Mrs. Earl's Delalor Banjo Bluespec of Iradell (by Comiston Bluespec Nicky out of Delalor Mitzi Maid). Also pictured was Mrs. Milton Fox with three Australian Terriers. This breed was recognized by the AKC in 1960, the year following the Silky Terrier's acceptance.

"The first of her kind in Colorado" read the article in the *Rocky Mountain News* of December 16, 1957. Pictured was Mindy, owned by Mr. and Mrs. James McMillan, who had been trying for more than a year to obtain a Silky.

In January 1958 a Redondo Beach, California, newspaper pictured Mrs. Robert McPhail with the Australian import Tibet Cheryl (by Tibet Marquis out of Tibet Bambi), owned by Mr. and Mrs. L. J. Keating. Mrs. McPhail was taking care of the Keating's Silky while they were visiting in Idaho. Mrs. McPhail had no idea what furor she was to create when she sent them the following wire, which included her address: "Four girls, two boys. All fine. Mrs. Robert McPhail."

Within a half hour her phone was jumping off the hook. Associated Press . . . Los Angeles metropolitan papers . . . Long Beach papers . . . the Japanese Embassy . . . everybody was calling to hear about the sextuplets. And how was Mrs. McPhail feeling? "Oh fine. Do you want to come and see the puppies?" The cause of the excitement was Tibby and her six newborn pups. Since the Keatings were fond of the dog and anxious about the delivery, Mrs. McPhail decided it was only proper they should receive prompt word about the birth. Hence the telegram. How did Mrs. McPhail feel about the excitement? "Well, it was fun, in a way." And if it ever happens again? "I'll make sure I mention they're puppies."

The Associated Press had got word of the telegram and alerted the local newspapers. There was no explanation of how the Japanese embassy became involved.

One of the early Australian imports, Aldoon Countess Candy, born in 1955 (by Glenboig Tim out of Aldoon Lassie). She was bred by Ivy Milne and owned by Bill and Beverly Lehnig. She became a champion soon after American Kennel Club recognition of the breed and is pictured here in her Best of Breed win at the 1960 Westminster Kennel Club show.

The *Los Angeles Times* of March 26, 1958, pictured Robert Cooley's daughter Cynthia and three of their Silky Terriers. They and Australian Terriers were featured in the accompanying article as rare breeds to be exhibited at the Glendale Kennel Club show the following Sunday.

Beverly and Bill Lehnig were pictured with their Australian import Aldoon Countess Candy (by Glenboig Tim out of Aldoon Lassie) and two of her pups in a feature article in the Louisville, Kentucky, *Evening News* in 1958. In June 1961 Beverly became the first Silky Terrier breed columnist in the monthly *Pure-Bred Dogs/American Kennel Gazette* magazine. She continued in this capacity for twenty years.

Isabel Rowley was pictured with two of her Silky Terriers in the *Long Beach Independent* newspaper on June 22, 1958.

The first Silky Terriers in West Virginia were announced in an article in the *West Virginian* on September 11, 1958. They were owned by Mr. and Mrs. Howard Colvin. Featured were Karmel Kim (by Kanimbla Sir Potch out of Kanimbla Zsa Zsa) and her litter of three, Sunfair Cindy Lou, Susie Q and Sonny Boy, sired by D'Under Beau Ganymede.

The *San Francisco Examiner* on October 26, 1958, featured the breed and pictured Howard Jensen's Waratah Winsome Winner (by Redway Lord Teasel out of Donny Brook Topsy). This bitch graced the cover of *Dog World* magazine in July 1959 in celebration of the American Kennel Club's recognition of the breed.

Louisiana's first Silky Terriers were those of Suzanne Link of New Orleans. They were featured in the Sunday newspaper supplement *Dixie* on December 14, 1958. Miss Link was pictured with Kanimbla Lady Jennifer (by Kanimbla Sir Potch out of Kanimbla Susan II) and Mad Manor Tiny Tim (by Redway Senor Willie out of Rofter Susie). Also pictured were two of their pups. The article told how it had taken exactly two years for Miss Link to obtain her first Silky in November 1956.

The final newspaper publicity prior to American Kennel Club recognition was in the *Reno Evening Gazette,* April 14, 1959. Pictured was Shirley McCormick with two bitches imported from Australia, Aldoon Lynde (by Glenboig Dison out of Aldoon Susie) and Totham Princess Audrey (by Stroud John Thomas out of Totham Princess Mary Anne).

Additional important exposure for the breed was gained by the increasing numbers of Silkys entered in the Miscellaneous class. The Miscellaneous class acts, primarily, as a showcase for rare breeds.

The class consists of a number of specified rare breeds. These are breeds that are recognized in other countries but not considered to be sufficient in number to warrant separate breed classification by the American Kennel Club. There are only two classes to enter: one for dogs and one for bitches. The entrants compete for first through fourth place, but the winners of these classes do not compete against each other for best in the Miscellaneous class. The winners receive pink ribbons for first in the classes—not the traditional blue ribbons awarded in regular class competition. There is no further competition in the show for the Miscellaneous class winners.

When Silky Terriers were being shown in this class they were competing with Akitas, Australian Heelers (now called Australian Cattle Dogs), Australian Kelpies, Australian Terriers, Border Collies, Chinese Crested Dogs, German Drathaars (now called German Wirehaired Pointers), Shih Tzus, Soft-coated Wheaten Terriers, Spinoni Italiani, Vizslas, Russian Owtchars, and Rhodesian Ridgebacks.

A number of California fanciers began entering their Silky Terriers in the Miscellaneous class in early 1955. The two-day, benched Golden Gate Kennel Club winter dog show is a popular spectator event in the San Francisco Bay area. At benched shows the dogs are on platforms, called benches, during the the entire day for everyone to view. At that time a great many shows were benched. Most shows are now unbenched. This means the dogs are not required to remain after competition in their breed.

In January 1955 Robert Garrett's Redway Splinter's Boy (by Wexford Pogo out of Brenhill Splinters) was the first Silky Terrier ever entered at the Golden Gate show. The other two entries in the Miscellaneous class were Rhodesian Ridgebacks. Then, as now, there was considerable publicity on radio and television and in the press, and as a result these two rare breeds were star attractions at the show. Just one year later the Silky Terrier entry at this show had increased to fourteen.

Toward the end of 1955 Silky Terriers were being entered in shows in other parts of the country. More and more breed pioneers joined in the concerted effort to popularize their breed. By 1959, when they became the 113th breed eligible to receive AKC championship points, Silky Terriers had been entered in 306 shows in the Miscellaneous class. It is estimated that between four and five hundred Silky Terriers had been imported by this time—a dramatic increase since that November 28, 1954, *This Week Magazine* cover picture.

Delalor Banjo Bluespec of Iradell, born in 1954 (by Comiston Bluespec Nicky out of Delalor Mitzi Maid). He was an adult import from Australia by Mrs. N. Clarkson Earl and later became a champion. This picture was the model for the Iradell Trophies offered by Mrs. Earl. He was bred by Mrs. N. Delaney.   *William Brown*

The dog that was to become the first American Kennel Club Silky Terrier champion: Milan Chips of Iradell (by Aus. Ch. Emeraldale Timothy out of Milan Lindy Lou). He was born in Australia in 1957 and imported by Mrs. N. Clarkson Earl from his breeder, Alan Miles.
                                                                                                 William Brown

Four of these imports were very influential in establishing the breed in the United States. Two of them, imported by Robert Cooley, are Aus. Ch. Bowenvale Murray and Aus. Ch. Kelso Lady Susan. Their influence comes down through their son, Ch. Coolaroo Sir Winston, and his son, Ch. Silkallure Casanova. The others are Ch. Wexford Pogo and Brenhill Splinters, imported by Peggy and Merle Smith. With them the influence comes down through various sons and daughters. Pictures and pedigrees of these four imports appear in Chapter 15.

Pioneer breeders in the United States whose dogs were included in the initial group of Silky Terriers registered with the American Kennel Club were Phyllis Buchanan and Suzanne Richardson, Buchrich; Vivien Chamberlain, Greenhills; Robert Cooley, Coolaroo; Florence Dahlstrom, Chota; Consuelo V. Earl, Iradell; Marjorie Edwards, Mara; Robert Garrett and Thomas Fromm, Sangate; Pat Huntington, Zelma; Howard Jensen, D'Under; Bill and Beverly Lehnig, Rebel; Mrs. John Morrison, Mad Manor; James and Henrietta Moss, Artarmon and Tumut; Erica Nicholls, Sarszegi; Lucille Tindall Preston, Fair Dinkum; Nettie Simmons, Clavons; Merle and Peggy Smith, Redway; Roland and Betty Stegeman, Waratah; and Martha and Geoffrey Sutcliffe, Kanimbla.

The Australian and New Zealand prefixes of Silky Terriers that comprised the foundation stock in America were Aldoon, Araluen, Barnbrae, Bindaboo, Bouden, Bowenvale, Brenhill, Coogee, Creiben, Delalor, Deloraine, Donny Brook, Ellwyn, Elysium, Glenbrae, Glenhaven, Glenlivet, Greengarth, Greenridge, Guildford, Ivy Thorn, Janricka, Kelso, Kendoral, Koolamina, Laang, Lignum, Lorangwyn, Mabrouka, Milan, Mira Belle, Nephthytis, Peteena, Prairie, Punchbowl, Rodleen, Rofter, Roscarberry, Stockport, Stroud, Sunbur, Tecoona, Tibet, Totham, Travelon, Viona, Wattle Dell, Westport, Wexford, Winsome and Zelburn.

3

The Modern
Silky Terrier
in America

THE FIRST American Kennel Club show at which Silky Terriers were eligible to compete for championship points was held July 4, 1959—Independence Day!—and by year's end eight had become champions. Four were owned by Consuelo Vanderbilt Earl, of Iradell Kennels in Connecticut, who was already well known for her top-winning Skye Terriers. She was very helpful as an intermediary between the American Kennel Club and the Silky Terrier Club of America in its quest for breed recognition. The first AKC champions were her Milan Chips of Iradell and Milan Jenny Wren of Iradell, imports from Australia. During those first six months Chips pioneered Group placements by the breed. He placed in ten Groups.

The other new champions in 1959 were Delalor Banjo Bluespec of Iradell and Aldoon Countess Candy, both Australian imports, as well as Iradell Peak A Boo, Coolaroo Janmar Marko, Coolaroo Sir Winston and Redway David, all American bred.

One of the first American Kennel Club Silky Terrier champions, Coolaroo Janmar Marko (by Creiben Michael John out of Coolaroo Star). Bred by Robert Cooley, owned by Martin and Jan Turner.

Ch. Shaw's Sapphire (on the left), who became a champion in 1961, with her six-month-old litter sired by Ch. Redway Lord Michael. They all became champions. They are Ackline's Belle of Sapphire, Ackline's Joy of Sapphire and Ackline's Samson of Sapphire, bred by Edna Ackerman.

Pictured at eight months of age is another early champion, Maurie Lady Rita, the winner of Best of Breed at the Silky Terrier Club of America's first match, judged by Mrs. C. Bede Maxwell in 1960. This Silky Terrier (by Ch. Wexford Pogo out of Mitry Lady Mandy) was bred and owned by Rinaldo Navarro.

Pictured in Australia at eight months of age is future Ch. Rockwood Valma (by Swaledale James out of Milan Milady). She was bred by Frank Longmore. W. A. (Fred) Wheatland, author of the out-of-print Australian publication *The Australian Terrier/The Australian Silky Terrier*, was the owner of her sire. She was imported in 1964 by James and Henrietta Moss.

Frank Longmore

Group, STCA Specialty Best of Breed and Iradell Trophy winner Ch. Silkallure Casanova (by Ch. Coolaroo Sir Winston out of Boridoon's Silkie Sullivan). Bred and owned by Victor and Mona Bracco. Casanova is the sire of two Best in Show winners.

Consuelo Earl inaugurated the first annual award for Silky Terriers, the Iradell Trophy. It was won the first year by Ch. Coolaroo Sir Winston, bred by Robert Cooley and owned by Fred and Susan Stern. The trophy was donated by Mrs. Earl, through the Silky Terrier Club of America, until 1971, when she disbanded her kennel. Since then it has been offered by the club. It honors the Silky with the most Best of Breed wins during the year, based on the number of championship points awarded at each show.

During 1960, the first full year of registrations, sixteen Silky Terriers became champions. The imports were Wexford Pogo, Kendoral Robyn, Milan Heather of Iradell, Prairie Joie, Koolamina Aussie, Milan Babs, Milan Silver Princess of Iradell, Kendoral Peter, and Milan Blue Peke of Iradell. The American-bred titlists were Mara's Silver Bob, Mad Manor Blue Breeze, Redway Lord Michael, Rebel Taffeta Ruffles, Redway Beau Brummell, Fair Dinkum Maverick, and Tumut's Lady Jan.

By 1978 the annual number of new champions had reached one hundred, and it continues to increase each year. And since relatively few Silky Terriers have been imported since the late 1950s, nearly all champions are American bred. More than two thousand have become champions. The breed ranks in the vicinity of fiftieth in popularity among the 130 breeds registered with the American Kennel Club, based on yearly registrations.

WESTMINSTER WINNERS

Wins at the prestigious Westminster Kennel Club show in New York City have always been much sought after. It was a proud day for pioneer breeders Bill and Beverly Lehnig when their Ch. Aldoon Countess Candy, handled by Beverly, was the first Silky to win Best of Breed there in 1960. This same year Candy was also the winner of the Iradell Trophy. Candy's daughter, Ch. Rebel Taffeta Ruffles, won the trophy in 1961.

Mrs. Earl's Ch. Milan Miss Sandra of Iradell was the first to place in the Toy Group at Westminster with a Group 4 in 1964. Ch. Silkallure Casanova, bred and owned by Victor and Mona Bracco, was the Best of Breed winner in 1966 and 1968 and captured a Group 4 in 1966. He was the winner of the Iradell Trophy in 1965, 1966 and 1967. It wasn't until 1986 that another Silky placed in the Group there. This was Ch. Dawnwind's Am I Blue, bred by Lucy Reynolds,

Ch. Ackline's Gin Gin Keg O'Luck, a multiple Group winner in the mid-1960s (by Ch. Delalor Banjo Bluespec of Iradell out of Ch. Shaw's Sapphire). Bred and owned by Edna Ackerman, she was handled for her owner by Tom Gately. *Gilbert*

Pictured at seven years of age is Ch. Silti Tumbleweed Pete (by Ch. Redway For Pete's Sake out of Ch. Silti's Dame Ditto), bred and owned by Mary T. Estrin, co-owned by Peggy Smith. *Newell*

Specialty Best of Opposite Sex winner Ch. Casa De Casey Mate O' The Mist (by Ch. Silkallure Casanova out of Silkallure Molly Brown). Bred by N. L. and W. Johnson, Jr., and owned by Richard and Jeanette Harper. *Ludwig*

Group-winning Ch. Dawnwind's Am I Blue (by Koonoona Independence Bo Bo out of Dawnwind's Liza of Ronco), was a Westminster winner in 1986. Bred by Lucy Reynolds and owned by Phyllis Tabler and Judy and Rebecca Kelsey. *John Ashbey*

Group and Specialty Best of Breed winner Ch. Redway Danny Boy O'Wexford (by Ch. Silky Acres Dandy Dude out of Ch. Redway Wexford Peter's Poppy), shown competing in the Toy Group at the Westminster Kennel Show at two years of age. Bred by Peggy Smith and owned by her and Eleanor Franceschi. *Callea*

also winning a Group 4. His owners are Phyllis Tabler and Judy and Rebecca Kelsey.

Casanova's son, Ch. Royaline Don Juan of Casanova, owned by Robert and Gloria Farron and bred by Mr. and Mrs. Bracco, was the winner of the Iradell Trophy in 1974 and 1975. He was Best of Breed at Westminster for a record three times, in 1973, 1974 and 1976. His Westminster record was equaled by William and Stephany Monteleone's Ch. Fawn Hill Lucknow Sweet N'Sour, bred by Verna Tucker, with Best of Breed honors there in 1983, 1985 and 1987, always handled by Stephany.

Peggy Smith is the only breeder of three Westminster Best of Breed Silky Terriers: Elsa Vinisko's Ch. Redway Lord Michael in 1962, her own Ch. Redway For Pete's Sake in 1975 and Ch. Redway Danny Boy O'Wexford in 1978. All were owner handled.

A complete listing of Westminster Kennel Club Best of Breed Silky Terriers appears in Chapter 13.

NATIONAL SPECIALTY WINNERS

The Silky Terrier Club of America held its first National Specialty show in San Mateo, California, in 1961, with twenty-eight Silky Terriers in competition. The Best of Breed winner was Ch. Waratah Walkabout, bred by Betty Stegeman and owned by Dorothy Lane. Best of Opposite Sex at this and the next two Specialties was the imported Ch. Bowenvale Margie, bred by Bowenvale kennels and owned by Fred and Susan Stern.

The following year, in Long Beach, California, the Silky entry jumped to forty-seven. The judge was Percy Roberts. It is not often that a Specialty Best of Breed is won by a dog at his first show, but it happened that day. The soon-to-become champion Billabong Tiny Tim, handled by his novice owner, Lee Shane, won the top award. Few terriers, or novice handlers, would have shown the composure of these two—Tiny Tim had been attacked by a large dog shortly before entering the ring.

The Specialty in Chicago in 1965 saw another class dog win Best of Breed. The judge was again Percy Roberts. This win finished the championship of Silkallure Casanova. He and Billabong Tiny Tim were half-brothers, both sired by Ch. Coolaroo Sir Winston.

Ch. Fawn Hill The Soroban was the first two-time top winner at the Specialty with his wins in 1968 and 1969. On both occasions

The 1962 Silky Terrier Club of America Specialty Best of Breed winner from the classes, soon to become Ch. Billabong Tiny Tim (by Ch. Coolaroo Sir Winston out of Coolaroo Lady Penny). Bred by Thora Sosinsky, owned by Lee and Julia Shane.

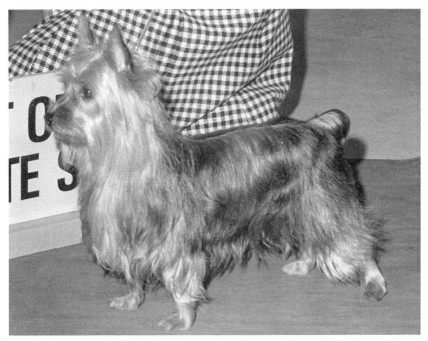

Ch. Soblu My Fancy (by Ch. Midland's Fancy Frankie out of Ch. Just a Smidgen of Dixie), whose Specialty wins retired the three-time-win Ch. Midland's Jan's Wendy Anne Trophy offered for Best of Opposite Sex. She was bred by Robert Davis and owned by Peggy Smith.

Graham

Ch. Redway For Pete's Sake (by Ch. Gem-G's Kool Hand Luke out of Ch. Soblu My Fancy). Bred and owned by Peggy Smith. *Francis*

45

Group and STCA Specialty Best of Opposite Sex winner Australian import Ch. Lylac Jan (by Leroy Misty out of Aldoon Wendy Ann). Bred by Nancy Glynn and owned by Carmen Cananzi.

A trio of champions: On the left is Ch. Silti's Blu Dimon Deb (by Ch. Silti's Joy Boy out of Silti's Jelli Bean Junior). In the center is Ch. Silti's Joy Boy (by Ch. Clavons Blue Rain out of Ch. Coolaroo Dame Wintiki). Both bred and owned by Mary T. Estrin. On the right is Ch. Coolaroo Dame Wintiki (by Coolaroo Lord Arbie out of Coolaroo Miss Susie). Bred by Robert Cooley and owned by Mary T. Estrin.   *Mills*

he was handled by his breeder, Verna Tucker. He was also the first Silky Terrier to be breeder/owner-handled to this win.

There have been three more two-time winners of the top spot: Ch. Lu-Jon's Lord Cagney of Tunney in 1970 and 1971, owned by Helen Thompson and John Lusk, handled by Don Thompson; Ch. Lylac Blue Prince in 1973 and 1974, owned by Ed and Marjorie Howard, handled by Jim Henderson; and Ch. Weeblu's Trailblazer of Don-El in 1980 and 1981, owner handled by Florence Males.

In 1968 Ed and Elinor Morrison, owners of Ch. Maurie Tuppence, a daughter of Ch. Wexford Pogo, offered the first Silky Terrier Club of America challenge trophy—the Ch. Wexford Pogo Memorial Trophy for Best of Breed. The condition was that, for permanent possession, the same owner must win three Specialty Bests of Breed, not necessarily with the same dog.

Eighteen years later William and Stephany Monteleone retired the trophy with their third consecutive Specialty Best of Breed in 1986. These three wins were with their Ch. Fawn Hill Lucknow Sweet N'Sour, bred by Verna Tucker and handled by Stephany.

The Best of Breed and Best of Opposite Sex winners at all Silky Club of America National Specialties are listed in Chapter 13.

BEST IN SHOW SILKY TERRIERS

The first American Best in Show win by a Silky Terrier was in May 1967 at the Upper Potomac Valley Kennel Club show in Maryland. At this show Ch. Midland's Jan's Wendy Anne was handled to the victory by Carmen Cananzi, her breeder and owner. In her honor he offered the second challenge trophy, the Ch. Midland's Jan's Wendy Anne Trophy for the Best of Opposite Sex at Specialties; it carried the same three-time win stipulation. This trophy was retired in 1971 by Peggy Smith, who handled her Ch. Soblu My Fancy to the third of her four consecutive wins. Fancy was bred by Robert Davis and was a granddaughter and great-granddaughter of Ch. Wexford Pogo.

Wendy Anne's sire, the imported Ch. Koonoona Bo Bo, became the second Best in Show winner at the Macomb County Kennel Club show in Michigan in 1968. He, too, was owned and handled by Carmen Cananzi.

The first multiple Best in Show Silky, winning two in 1968, was

A litter of four champions, bred by Florence Males. *Left to right:* Weeblu's Wee One-Der of Joy, Weeblu's Princess Powder Puff, Weeblu's Windsong of Joy and Weeblu's Candyman Can. They were sired by Ch. Silti's Joy Boy out of Ch. Silkallure Wee One.   *Jim Lawson*

At a California show in 1973 Australian all-breed judge Cameron Milward chose three winners, all sired by Ch. Gem-G's Kool Hand Luke. On the left is Winners Dog, Avan Blue Devil's Advocate, owned by Sue Avanzino; next is Best of Winners and Best of Opposite Sex, Lylac Dawn's Dodie Baby, owned and bred by Will and Rachael Cabral. Their dam was Ch. Lylac Windy Dawn. Both became champions. On the right is the Best of Breed winner, Ch. Redway For Pete's Sake (out of Ch. Soblu My Fancy), bred and owned by Peggy Smith.

In the center is Ch. Larkspurs Blue Chip (by Ch. Silti's Joy Boy out of Ch. Ronco's Skat Dancer). On either side are his daughters, Ch. Larkspurs Tuckaway Sugar Bebe and Ch. Larkspurs Tuckaway Angel (out of Ronco's Christy Love of Jason). They are owned by Carolyn and James Stewart.

Thornton

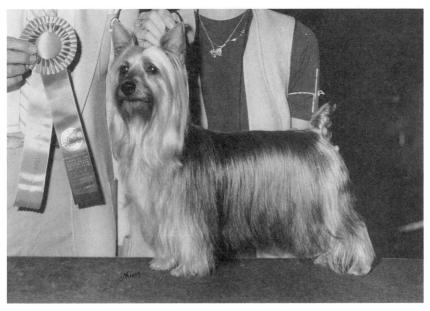

Ch. Koala's Katch Me If You Kan, a Specialty Best of Breed and Group winner (by Ch. Koala Toy Boy, CD, out of Ch. Koala's Lovable Tinkerbelle). Bred and owned by Doreen and Jason Gross. *Missy*

Ch. Friant's Crystal Champagne (by Quantas and Friants Al Gator out of Friant's Sugar Baby). Bred by Cindy Friant and owned by Dorothy Pritchard.

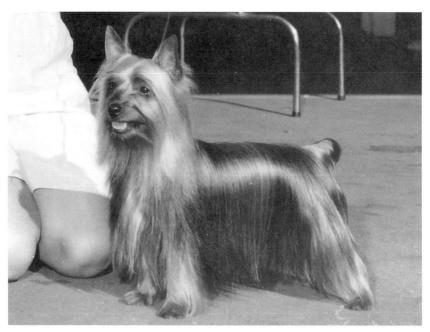

Group and Iradell Trophy winner Ch. Tri-K Marina's Kalypso Kali (by Ch. Marina's Dallas out of Ch. Kirstin's Kasse of Cassanova). Bred by Kriste and Kriss Griffin and owned by Kriss and Kirstin Griffin.   *Missy*

Ch. Hargill's Jolly Jamboree, bred and owned by Harriett Gill. He was handled by Houston Clark.

The 1970s saw more of these top awards being won by Silky Terriers. Ch. Lylac Blue Prince, bred in Australia by Nancy Glynn, won six Bests in Show. He was owned by Ed and Marjorie Howard and handled by Jim Henderson. Prince was the winner of the Iradell Trophy for an unprecedented four years, beginning in 1970.

During this same period Robert and Gloria Farron's Ch. Roya-line Don Juan of Casanova was awarded a record-setting seven Bests in Show. Ch. Cantell Heard A Rumor, bred by Fred Pierson and owned by Mary Lee Hendee and Dolores Streng, came close to this record with six Bests in Show in 1981 and 1982.

In 1982 Ch. Weeblu's Trailblazer of Don El equaled the record seven Bests in Show and, in 1985, set a new record by winning an eighth. He was a three-time winner of the Iradell Trophy. Trailblazer was bred by Don and Helen Thompson and always handled by his owner, Florence Males. She also handled his sire, Ch. Weeblu's Blaze of Joy, bred and owned by her, to two Bests in Show. His second top award was from the Veteran's class.

Only two Silky Terrier bitches have taken all-breed Best in Show awards. In 1985, eighteen years after that first Silky Terrier Best in Show by Ch. Midland's Jan's Wendy Anne, another bitch gained this high award. William and Stephany Monteleone's Ch. Fawn Hill Lucknow Sweet N'Sour was twice honored with the top win. She was handled, as always, by Stephany. She was also an Iradell Trophy recipient.

Verna Tucker has the distinction of being the only breeder of two all-breed Best in Show Silky Terriers: the above-mentioned Sweet N'Sour and her own Ch. Fawn Hill The Donnybrook, co-bred by Eleanor Norton. Donnybrook was only seven when he met an untimely death in 1983, but the pedigrees of many recent champions often have his name appearing more than once, thereby indicating his influence on the breed.

A complete listing of all-breed Best in Show Silky Terriers appears in Chapter 13.

BREEDERS' HALL OF FAME

Numerous breeders of Silky Terriers in this country and abroad are to be commended for the vast improvement in the breed during

Ch. Larkspurs Joyous Noel (by Ch. Larkspurs Blue Waggin, CDX, out of Larkspur Whispered Rumor). Bred by Carolyn Stewart and Sally Dylewski and owned by Frank and Carla Fyock and Carolyn Stewart.

Group, Specialty Best of Breed and All Toy Breeds Best in Show winner Ch. Tru Blu Ziggy Stardust (by Ch. Tru Blu Rumors A'Cookin' out of Ch. Larkspurs Rustle of Taffeta). Bred and owned by Linda Mowrer. *Missy*

Ch. Centarra's Trivial Pursuit, a Group, Specialty Best of Breed and Iradell Trophy winner (by Tak'Ope Tu-Shu out of Ch. Mercer's Muffy Mischievous). Bred and owned by Pam and Paul Laperruque. *Missy*

the past thirty years. American breeders who have bred five or more champions are listed below, along with their kennel prefixes.

Edna Ackerman, Acklines
Janet Aslett, Aslett
Wilma Awana, Franmas
Larry and Carolyn Batten, Silblu
Norma Baugh, Amron
Myrtle Baumgartner, Creek Run
David Beckhoff, Joda
William Betchley, Bifrost
Louise Bialek, Dunar
Mona Bracco, Casa De Casey
Vickie Bratton, Tumbelles
Jimmy Bridges, Kinloch
Lillian Brinkerhoff, Brinkerhoff
Mary Brisco, Daklyn
K. F. Brown, Tuckaway
Angeline Burgio, Lou-Ann
Arlene Byers, Koobala
Carmen Cananzi, Midland
Mildred and Bill Carlstrom, Sami-D
Joan Caspersen, Sundowner
Aleida Castetter, Tails-West
Arline Clark, Nukara
Joe and Donna Clas, Jazzbo
J. S. and H. F. Claus, Bucmar
James and Elizabeth Click, Cormat
Chris Colman, Ronco
Phyllis Cook, Pycosite
Robert Cooley, Coolaroo
Louise Coviello, Cha-Lu
Rene Daniels, Re-Dan
Edna and Robert Davis, Soblu
Rita Dawson, Silwynd
William Deller, Austral
Ruth Di Stefano, Lakewind
Charles Dunn, Silkallure
Lou Durocher, Lu-Jon
Consuelo Earl, Iradell

Harry Eastham, Ceejay
Robert and Lee Easton, Easton
Anne and Peter Edgar, Admiral
Earl Edge, Damae
Carol Eldridge, Windhaven
Jean Eliker, Saturn
Jeane Ems, Hi-Jinx
Laurie Ericson, Marina
Mary Estrin, Silti
Robert and Gloria Farron, Royaline
Diane Fenger, Tara Lara
Bernadette Fletcher, Glen Row
Zara and James Flood, Billabong
Eleanor Franceschi, Wexford
Pat Gesler, Jampat
Harriett Gill, Hargill
Kriss and Kriste Griffin, Tri-K
Doreen and Jason Gross, Koala
Ethel Haley, Tak'Ope
Elizabeth Harrison, Austi
Ron Hartright-Leighton, Ronnsown
Barbara Heckerman, Wyncrest
Fern Hemmert, Spinner
Mary Lee Hendee, Cantell
Dorothy Hicks, Cypress Mi-Ohn
Henry Hinojosa, Shani
Alice Hively, Queen's Own
John and Jean Hoover, Starho
Gene and Paula Huff, Chrisbonli
Rose Jackerson, Rolen
Amy and Jean Jones, Spennymoor
Joene Kelly, Ridgewyn
Janice Klaus, Centella
Florence Kotecki, Flo-Ko

Specialty Best of Breed and Group winner Ch. Sun Dance's Ragtime (by Ch. Cantell Heard A Rumor out of Cantell Tongue in Cheek, CD). Bred and owned by Shirley Worley.   *Phoebe*

Group-winning Ch. Amron's Hug-A-Bear (by Ch. Marina's Dallas out of Ch. Amron's Crystal Pistol). Bred and owned by Norma Baugh.

Ch. Lylac Blue Prince (by Lylac Playboy out of Prairie Dail), an Australian import, was a Specialty Best of Breed winner with six Bests in Show. He was also an Iradell Trophy winner. Bred by Nancy Glynn and owned by Marjorie and Edward Howard. *Ludwig*

Ch. Anahab's Up and Adam, pictured at fourteen months (by Ch. Thaddeus Jude of Westchester out of Dicar of Mar J's Little Cindy). Bred by Diane Bushman and owned by Margaret and Richard Gagliardi.

Richard La Barre, Mavrob
Pam and Paul Laperruque,
 Centarra
Helen Larson, Keneko
Beverly Lehnig, Rebel
J. J. Lemley, Pennybottom
Arlene Lewis, Jenolan
Laura Lola, Lolita
C. and E. Lubrano, Belle Cane
John Lusk, Lu-Jon
Victoria Macy, Elmvale
Diane Magnuson, Lapsitter
Jon and Kay Magnussen,
 Kiku
Florence Males, Weeblu
Raymond and Irma Marshall,
 Alcamar
D. and M. Mathers, Dumane
Janet Matthews, Sonnyvale
Angelica Mazzarella, Dreaman
Stephany and William
 Monteleone, Lucknow
William Morse, Morsilk
James Moss, Tumut and
 Artarmon
Linda Mowrer, Tru Blu
Marie Nelson, Seablu
Oen and Sue Nelson, Sunel
Delbert and Eleanor Noble,
 Noble
Eleanor Norton, Dariuswood
Susan O'Rear, Luxa
Mildred Pequignot, Austral
Judy and George Pesa, Mill
 Creek
Carolyn Pfeiffer, Trupence
Len and Lettie Pilley,
 Moonfleet
Julie Pizzirulli, Safire
Betty Receveur, Dixie

Donna and Steve Renton,
 Tawney Mist
Ivy Rogers, Jenini
Louise Rosewell, Rosewell
John and Maureen Sass,
 Merrigang
Phyllis Schneider, Blu-N-Tan
Michael and Suellen Shanker,
 Anova
Nettie Simmons, Clavons
Roger and Dawn Slowi, Aruma
Peggy Smith, Redway
Virginia Smith, Vamaro
Beverly Stanley, Sterling
Arlene Steinle, Tara Lara
Fred and Susan Stern,
 Silkallure
Carolyn and James Stewart,
 Larkspur
Mary Stahl, Timberly
Dee Stoddard, Roy-Dee
Karen Stopa, Kilee
Delores Streng, Cantell
Martha Sutcliffe, Kanimbla
Mary Thalheimer, Marle
Howard Thomas, Starline
Don and Helen Thompson,
 Don-El
Ann and Mary Tolley, Mar-An
Verna Tucker, Fawn Hill
Murtle Turnage, Rosewell
Elsa Vinisko, Elmikes
Margaret Vitone, Toiboi
Patricia Walton, Silky Acres
Lynn Waters, Merry Moppet
Gwenna Weymouth, Wym-Wey
Mary Wilson, Vamaro
Janean Wylie, Avonwyck
Betty Young, Larrakin
Alice Zahnd, Mistiblu

Aus. Ch. Hillside Bella Marie, a Best in Toy Group winner in the early 1950s in Victoria, Australia. Bred and owned by the Norman Wenker family. Mr. Wenker is an all-breed judge.

4

The Silky Terrier Around the World

O VER THE YEARS Silky enthusiasts have introduced the breed in many countries. The descriptions that follow chronicle the Silky Terrier's growth around the world.

AUSTRALIA

American interest in the Silky Terrier during the mid-1950s spurred considerable activity in the breed in their homeland. It had been many years since any breed club catered to Australian Silky Terriers, as they have been called there since 1956. Then, as now, most Silky Terrier breeders were located in Victoria and New South Wales. Thanks mainly to the efforts of Frank A. Longmore, an all-breed judge, the Australian Silky Terrier Club of Victoria was organized in March 1958. The Australian Silky Terrier Club of New South Wales was formed in December 1959.

That same year, with American Kennel Club recognition of the breed imminent, one of the first orders of business by the newly

Aus. Ch. Stroud John William, born in 1953 (by Stroud John Mark Anthony out of Stroud Vivien Leigh), was bred by Mrs. Birkin-O'Donnell. She and her brother, Mr. Birkin of the Totham prefix, bred Silkys from the late 1940s into the early 1960s in New South Wales, Australia.

Aus. Ch. Bowenvale Sir Rex, born in 1957 (by Aus. Ch. Bowenvale Billy out of Bowenvale Beauty). He was bred by Eric Fellows and owned by Miss E. Simper, of the Glen Elsa prefix, in Victoria, Australia.

Aus. Ch. Milan Tony at eighteen months of age. He was born in 1958 and was one of the first to win all-breed Bests in Show. He was bred and owned by Alan Miles of Victoria, Australia.

Aus. Ch. Clarkdale Wee Sante, born in 1961 (by Aus. Ch. Koolamina Sante out of Aus. Ch. Clarkdale Louise). Bred by Mrs. Naize Clark and owned by H. Morgan.

Aus. Ch. Koolamina Sante, born in 1957 (by Aus. Ch. Prairie Playboy out of Koolamina Gay Girl). He was bred by H. Patterson and owned by Mr. and Mrs. C. Budd of New South Wales, Australia. Sante was a Toy Group and Silky Specialty winner.

Aus. Ch. Rodleen Prince Tiger (by Aus. Ch. Auran Radiant Bimbo out of Aus. Ch. Princess Wendylu). He was an all-breed Best in Show winner in 1962 in Victoria, Australia. Bred by David Blewett and owned by J. Wilkinson.

Frank Longmore

Aus. Ch. Bouden Beau, born in 1960, a son of Aus. Ch. Milan Tony out of Bouden Louandy. He is pictured at nine months of age. He finished his championship two months later. He was bred by Miss E. J. Williams, in Victoria, and brought to New South Wales by Mrs. W. S. Greer, whose prefix was Greengarth. He and his sire contributed greatly to breed improvement.

Aus. Ch. Rodleen Salient, born in 1964 (by Aus. Ch. Tamworth Gay Spark out of Princess Cindylu), bred and owned by David Blewett. She was awarded the challenge certificate at the 1966 Melbourne Royal Show, in Victoria, Australia, by author Peggy Smith. She repeated the win the following year and was a multiple Toy Group winner.

formed Australian National Kennel Council was to compile a national Standard for the breed in that country. Working with a national Standard that was more stringent, particularly concerning size, the new specialist clubs were able to bring about considerable improvement in the breed within just a few years.

It took until the 1950s for Silky Terriers to hold their own in Toy Group competition. One of the first to gain widespread attention in the Group was Ch. Hillside Bella Marie, bred and owned by the Norman Wenker family. Her sire was their Ch. Kansas Kiwi and her dam was Hillside Melody. In her coverage of the 1953 Royal Melbourne show, canine journalist Mrs. C. Bede Maxwell wrote: "Best in Group honours were easily won by a beautiful English Champion Pomeranian, the Best Opposite Sex in Group award went to a 'glamour plus' top winning Pekingese bitch. The bitch honours were toughly contested by a superb Silky, Champion Hillside Bella Marie, put down in incredible bloom and showing to perfection. More than one ringsider 'had the money' on the Silky."

One of the first to win Toy Groups and multiple all-breed Best in Show honors was Ch. Milan Tony. Bred and owned by Alan Miles, Tony was born in 1958. His sire was Ch. Emeraldale Timothy and his dam was Blue Susan, two of the Milan Kennels' foundation stock. He sired more than two dozen champions and is behind most of the winning stock in Australia today.

Since then numerous Silky Terriers have taken Group and all-breed Best in Show awards. Some of them are pictured in this chapter.

CANADA

Marian Wait, now an all-breed judge in Canada, imported the first Silky Terrier to Canada in 1962. This was Maryanne Dolly, bred by Neva Seagly of Indiana. Dolly was by Am. Ch. Austral Prince Kirby out of Am. Ch. Aldoon Tinkerbelle, an import from Australia.

Marian later imported a dog and bitch from Nettie Simmons of Rhode Island. The dog was one of the first Canadian champions, Clavons Blue Valient (by Am. Ch. Kanimbla's Wee Kelso Kelly out of Am. Ch. Victoria Anastasia). The bitch was Clavons Blue Trinket (by Clavons Blue Brass Bound out of Kanimbla Lady Penelope). Another early Canadian champion was her import from Australia in 1966, Milan Rose Anne (by Aus. Ch. Milan Kelly out of Milan Blossom).

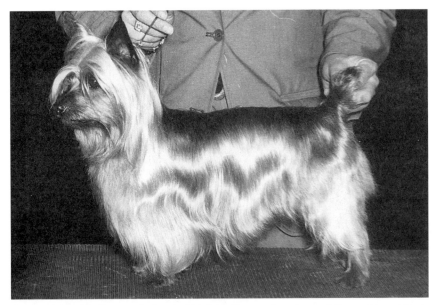

Can. and Am. Ch. Bonneen's Arunta Chieftain. He was the winner of three all-breed Bests in Show in Canada and one in the United States. *E. H. Frank*

Aus. Ch. Waiton Carbon Copy, born in 1972 (by Aus. Ch. Waiton Billy Boy out of Careff Countess Carina). He was a multiple Best in Specialty winner at shows held by the Australian Silky Terrier Club of New South Wales and a multiple Best Toy award-winner. He was bred by Mrs. R. V. Maher and owned by Jan Boyce, Nantiki Kennels.

Can. Ch. Hopeparks Naughty But Nice, born in 1985 (by Bama's Kiku's Wind Up Toy out of Shoshana's Butch Cassidy). She is also an Am. and Can. CDX and a Can. TDX. She is owned by Heather Somers of British Columbia, Canada.

Aus. Ch. Pennanji Belinda, born in 1977 (by Aus. Ch. Karribi Blue Glen out of Aus. Ch. Pennanji Mitzie). She was bred by J. R. Skippen and owned by Jan Boyce.

Aus. Ch. Adamanda Fabian, born in 1977 (by Aus. Ch. Careff Perhaps out of Aus. Ch. Adamanda Melody). Bred and owned by Ruth Bennett, he was Best of Breed at the 1980 Sydney Royal Show and an all-breed Best in Show winner. He sired more than fifteen champions. *Michael M. Trafford*

A young bitch, Northrise Silken Slipper (by Gimmonas Feet for Faigth Lennie out of Northrise Momentum), bred by Ena North of London, England. *Hartley*

Through Mrs. Wait's efforts the breed was recognized by the Canadian Kennel Club in 1965. It was called the Silky Toy Terrier until 1988, when the name was changed to Silky Terrier.

In 1987 Mrs. Wait was asked to judge in Brisbane, Australia. There was an unusually large entry due to the widespread knowledge that she had been responsible for establishing the breed in Canada. The Silky Terrier exhibitors hosted a wine and sandwich party in her honor to show their appreciation.

The only Silky Terrier to become a top winner in Canada is Am. and Can. Ch. Bonneen's Arunta Chieftain. His breeder, Darrell Jordon, and his owner, Joseph Medina, lived in California. His sire and dam were Australian imports, Tamworth Cal and Bonneen Blue Mist. The illustrious Aus. Ch. Milan Tony was Blu Mist's double grandsire.

In the late 1960s Silky fanciers Lu Durocher and John Lusk moved to Canada from southern California and Chieftain went with them. He had a noteworthy career and was handled to all his wins by Lu. He won three all-breed Bests in Show in Canada and one in the United States. In 1970 he was the top winner of the Toy breeds in Canada and the top winning Silky Terrier in the United States. He was the sire of seven American champions, including Ch. Lu-Jon's Lord Cagney of Tunney, who was Best of Breed at two Silky Terrier Club of America National Specialty shows.

A number of Silky Terriers have been imported to Canada from Australia and the United States, but the breed continues to be rare there.

GREAT BRITAIN

A few Silky Terriers were imported to Great Britain in the 1930s. *Hutchinson's Dog Encyclopaedia,* published in England in 1955, gives a brief description of the "Sydney Silky," noting it to be quite a new breed in Great Britain. It pictures Roimata Bon Ton, owned by a Mrs. Caskie, and describes this Silky as a prize winner at the Canterbury Kennel Club show in 1933. The kennel prefix indicates that the dog was bred in New Zealand.

The breed remained virtually unknown in Great Britain until the late 1970s, when a few were imported. The thought behind this was to introduce a long-coated breed that requires relatively simple grooming. Gaining popularity has proven to be a formidable task, since England's native breed, the smaller Yorkshire Terrier, which is similar in color and coat texture, is so well established and popular there. Undoubtedly British fanciers face the same problem experienced by the breed pioneers in the United States: the opinion of some is that Silky Terriers are simply "bad Yorkshire Terriers." It is true that a bad Yorkshire Terrier can resemble a Silky Terrier and that a bad Silky Terrier can be mistaken for a Yorkshire Terrier. However, a correct Silky Terrier, of proper size and coat length, cannot be mistaken for any other breed by knowledgeable fanciers or judges.

Among the first British Silkys were two imported by Barbara Garbett. One was the Holland-bred Apico Yatara Dutchboy (by Connalee Regal Supreme out of Dutch Ch. Kaylaw Samara, both from Australia). The other was also from Australia, Glenpetite Lolita (by Milan Tramp out of Glenpetite Ena).

During this same period Linda Stewart imported a bitch, Coolmine Dockan, from Ireland. Her sire and dam, Vasterbackens Debut and Albertina, were bred in Sweden. Miss Stewart also imported from Australia Glenpetite Wataboy, whose sire and dam were Milan Hugo and Aus. Ch. Galacksi Petite Susie.

The inaugural meeting of the Australian Silky Terrier Society was held in 1980. Joy Jolley, secretary of the club, has kept complete records of the breed, and these indicate that eleven have been imported, including one bitch in whelp. Registrations with the Kennel Club (U.K.) have been as follows: twenty-four in 1981, thirty-seven in 1982, forty-four in 1983, thirty-seven in 1984, sixty-nine in 1985, thirty-one in 1986, fifty-six in 1987, and twenty-five in 1988. Many of the all-breed kennel clubs provide classes for the breed, but Silkys are not eligible for challenge certificates. Their club has applied for championship status each year, but the required numbers have not yet been registered or exhibited.

When the author and Beverly Lehnig visited England in 1983, there were many Silkys of good quality entered at the Australian Silky Terrier Society's show. However, there was considerable variation in type, with some dogs having near black coats with what is best described as Irish Terrier red rather than rich tan. It was encouraging to read a critique, written in 1988 by an English breeder-judge, expressing the opinion that their Silkys are returning to the correct type such as was imported in the late 1970s.

A pair of British Silkys. On the left is Marshdae Koobor of Gerallyn (by Apico Archie of Marshdae out of Wybilena Kaarimba of Marshdae), bred by Ann Marshall; on the right is his daughter, Gerallyn Goondiwindi Princess (out of Keelham Miranda of Gerallyn), bred by Geraldine Tomlinson of Cheshire, England, owner of both.

71

EUROPE

Silky Terriers are shown in the Terrier Group at Fédération Cynologique Internationale shows and in most European countries.

Holland and Germany

Until 1961 Silky Terriers were unknown throughout most of Europe. That year, when traveling on business, Robert Cooley, of the Coolaroo Kennels in California, attended the Hofstad Dog Show in The Hague, Holland. There he met Anny Reijerink-Tibbe, of Holland (now Anny Hartman-Tibbe of Germany), who was exhibiting her Cairn Terriers.

As a result of their meeting she imported two Silkys to Europe. Both were bred by Robert Cooley and became international champions. The bitch was Coolaroo Karin (by Aus. Ch. Prairie Playboy out of Coolaroo Star). The dog was Coolaroo Pasja (by Aus. Ch. Bowenvale Murray out of Sunbur Cynthia). Mrs. Reijerink-Tibbe exhibited Silkys all over Europe and interest soon spread.

France

The first Silky Terriers in France were also from the Coolaroo Kennels. They were imported by Pierre Passerieux, Farmer's Kennels, whose first litter was born in 1965. Others Silkys have subsequently been imported from Australia and the United States.

Int. Ch. Vetzyme De La Colline De Lorette is a top winning Silky in France. His sire is Glen Petite Blue Patch, and his dam is Topaze. He was bred by Evelyne Pruvost and is owned by Odile Tremblay.

Sweden

An annual Nordic show is held in either Sweden, Norway or Finland, at which there is intercountry competition. Each best of breed is awarded the title Nordic Winner. The title Nordic Champion is awarded to those dogs that have completed championship requirements in all three countries. Anna Lisa and Elisabeth Westberg, Vasterbackens Kennels, were the first Silky Terrier breeders in Sweden. A professor at Stockholm University, traveling in Australia in 1965, bought a Silky bitch in whelp to Tauto Talisman Taurus (by

A top winning Silky Terrier in France *(at right)*, Int. Ch. Vetzyme De La Colline De Lorette, bred by Evelyne Pruvost and owned by Odile Tremblay. Pictured with him is a young bitch, Belle De jour De Malahia.

A top winner in Scandinavia, Int., Swed., Norw. and Fin. Ch. Softhair's Silver Air, bred by Britta Samuelsson of Sweden. He is heavily linebred to Aus., Swed. and Norw. Ch. Munbilla Rob Roy.

Int. and Nord. Ch. Samiras Harrax, bred and owned by Gunn-Britt Hjelm of Sweden. His sire is Aus., Nord. and Int. Ch. Adamanda Charwil, bred by Ruth Bennet of Australia. His dam is Samiras Ebonette.

Int. and Nord. Ch. Eraldo's Blueberry Pie (by Nord. Ch. Dulcannina Man in Blue out of Funny Dog's Regina). Bred and owned by Gunnel Odlare of Sweden.
Per Unden

Samiras Sir Yeppoon, pictured at eight months of age. He was born in June 1988, the year that tail docking was outlawed in Sweden and Norway. His breeder/owner is Gunn-Britt Hjelm.

A top winning bitch bred by Ann Lise Dedie of Switzerland. Fr., Lux., Mon. and Int. Ch. Mousseline St. Didier, owned by Mr. and Mrs. Guy David of France.

Aus. Ch. Koolamina High Top out of Tauto Dinky Di). The bitch was Aus. Ch. Coppice Checina Lady (by Aus. Ch. Bonneen Buster out of Kabakaul Charlotte Leslie). Checina Lady's litter was born at Vasterbackens Kennels, and she ultimately added the Swedish and Norwegian championship titles to her name.

The Westbergs were so attracted to the breed that they immediately imported a mature dog and bitch from Australia. The dog was Aus. Ch. Coolibah Cobbity (by Aus. Ch. Rodleen Boy Blue out of Aus. Ch. Madani Lady Fair). Cobbity also became a Swedish and Norwegian champion. The bitch was Booroondara Steffe (by Aus. Ch. Biggara Shay out of Aus. Ch. Kabakaul Cupid Lady). They whelped the first litter of their own breeding in 1965.

In 1966 Lisa Allrin, Lillgardens Kennels, imported Int. Ch. Coolaroo Gantine's Randy to Sweden from Anny Reijerink-Tibbe's Gantine Kennels in Holland. His sire was Aus. Ch. Bonneen Boz and his dam was Int. Ch. Coolaroo Karin. In 1968 she imported Casa de Casey's Venessa from Mona and Victor Bracco of California and bred her first litter. Venessa's dam was Merry Moppet. Mrs. Allrin later imported two more bitches from Mrs. Bracco. One was Casa De Casey's Venus, bred by Janean Wylie; her dam was Mabrob Fair Trina. The other was Casa De Casey's Miss Sweden, bred by Anthony Govatos and William Buell; her dam was Garona Silver Penny. All three, sired by the Bracco's homebred Ch. Silkallure Casanova, became international champions.

Gunn-Britt Hjelm arrived in Sweden in 1973 from Australia with two imports. The dog was Penannji Sonny Boy (by Aus. Ch. Munbilla Rob Roy out of Guruga Teena Maree). The bitch was Aus. Ch. Penannji Serena (by Aus. Ch. Guruga Rexies Image out of Stroud Lady Caroline).

Int. and Nord. Ch. Samiras Harrax, the Nordic Winner in 1979, was bred by Gunn-Britt Hjelm. His sire is Aus., Nord., and Int. Ch. Adamanda Charwil; his dam is Samiras Ebonette. He was shown three times in 1988 as a twelve-year-old Veteran and was Best of Breed each time, as well as twice being awarded Best Veteran in Show.

Int. Ch. Softhair's Silver Air was bred and owned by Britta Samuelsson. His sire is Swed. Ch. Gimona's Sunday Sam; his dam is Swed. Ch. Tanjagardens Kaljinka. In 1984 and 1985 he won the title of Nordic Winner. He is heavily linebred to Aus., Swed., and Norw. Ch. Munbilla Rob Roy, who was imported in 1972 by Hildur Renkaitis, Swedehills Kennel. Rob Roy was sired by Aus. Ch. Mi-

Falpala Arcibald (by Am. and Int. Ch. Centarra's Billy Th' Kid out of Centarra's Been Silver Kist). Bred and owned by Delia Morgotti Montanari, who is the first breeder of Silky Terriers in Italy. *Carlo Pozzoni*

Fin. Ch. Stenilja Diamantina at fifteen months of age (by Fin. Ch. Stenilja Buccaneer out of Fin. Ch. Bogunda Rose Marie). Owned and bred by Silja Valimaa-Koskimaa of Finland.

Aus. Ch. Karribi My Starlet, born in 1983 (by Aus. Ch. Karribi Jamie Boy out of Aus. Ch. Karribi Stargem). She is one of many top winning champions bred by Joan Geogeghan of Victoria, Australia.

Aus. Ch. Lylac Jak, born in 1985 (by Aus. Ch. Lylac S. Smiley out of Lylac Sunburnt Sal). He was reserve challenge dog at the 1988 Sydney Royal Show in New South Wales. He was bred by Nancy Glynn, who has been breeding Silky Terriers for almost thirty years. *Michael M. Trafford*

New Zealand and Aus. Ch. Bam's Boy of
Lakemba (by Wilsight Bam Bam out of
New Zealand and Aus. Ch. Adamanda
Honey Luv). Bred and owned by Jean and
Ray McKay of New Zealand, he was shown
in Australia by Ruth Bennett, the breeder
of his dam. He gained his Australian title
in twenty days. He was Best of Breed at
a world record seven Silky Specialty shows
and a winner of two all-breed Bests in
Show. *Michael M. Trafford*

Aus. Ch. Canaussie Casanova
(by Aus. Ch. Heatherset Fonzie
out of Canaussie Lady Jennie.
Bred by A. Caverley and B.
Ross-Smith and owned by Annette Collins.
Photography by Twigg

Aus. Ch. Allanette Miss Muf-
fett, born in 1984 (by Aus.
Ch. Heatherset Fonzie out of
Joyklis Lady Elsie). She won
the reserve challenge certificate at the 1987 Mel-
bourne Royal Show. Bred
and owned by Annette Col-
lins.
Photography by Twigg

lawn Malooka; his dam was Aus. Ch. Munbilla Miss Primm. He came out of retirement in 1978 and, from the Veterans class, won several Best of Breed awards. He also had the title of Nordic Winner.

Gunnel Odlare has had Silky Terriers since 1976. In 1988 she published the first book written about the breed in Swedish. She is president of the Swedish Silky Terrier Circle, founded in 1980, which has a membership of about 150. Her Int. and Nord. Ch. Eraldo's Blueberry Pie, bred and owned by her, is a top winner.

Between sixty and eighty Silky Terriers are born yearly in Sweden. In 1988 tail docking was outlawed in Sweden and Norway. The Swedish Kennel Club has instructed judges to ignore the carriage of the tails until the breed Standards have been changed to indicate how they should be carried.

Finland

The breed was introduced to Finland in 1972 by Curt Gerlins, Fayhill Kennel. His first Silky Terriers were from Vasterbackens Kennels in Sweden. In 1975 he imported a dog and a bitch from Australia. The dog was Aus. Ch. Adamanda Charwil, an all-breed Best in Show winner in his homeland. He went on to become an international and Nordic champion and sire of a number of Scandinavian champions. Charwil's sire was Behntoi Tiny Tim; his dam was Aus. Ch. Jernaise Trudy. The bitch was Lylac Honey Bun (by Lylac Blue Jeremy out of Lylac Honey Baby).

In 1973 Silja Valimaa-Koskimaa, Stenilja Kennel, imported a bitch from Lillgardens Kennel in Sweden. This was Fin. Ch. Lillgardens Blue Penny (by Swed. Ch. Lillgardens Muffi out of Int. and Nord. Ch. Casa De Casey's Venessa). In 1985 she imported Bogunda Rose Marie from Australia (by Aus. Ch. Lahinch Jim Jam out of Aus. Ch. Bogunda Prissy Missy). Rose Marie became a Finnish champion and was the Nordic Winner in 1986. She is the dam of Fin. Ch. Stenilja Diamantina. Diamantina's sire is Fin. Ch. Stenilja Buccaneer.

In 1988 the Silky Terrier Club of Finland was founded, with Mrs. Valimaa-Koskimaa as its first president.

Switzerland

In 1972 Ann Lise Dedie, St. Didier Kennel, imported, from France, the first Silky Terrier. She was Farmer's Voska (by Farmer's

Aus. Ch. Heatherset Fonzie, born in 1982 (by Aus. Ch. Kateena Thor out of Heatherset Tinkerbell). He was the challenge certificate winner at the 1987 Melbourne Royal Show. He was bred by Carol Dunn and is owned by Annette Collins of Victoria, Australia.

Photography by Twigg

Aus. Ch. Glorford the Stirrer, born in 1984 (by Aus. Ch. Idem Ragtime out of Tarawera Bettina). She was Best of Breed at the 1987 and 1988 Sydney Royal shows and Best of Opposite Sex in the Toy Group at the 1988 show. Bred by Reg Hitchens and owned by Jenny Smith.   *Terry Dorizas*

Aus. Ch. Kaylaw Letum Talk, born in 1982 (by Aus. Ch. Kaylaw Koomak out of Aus. Ch. Kaylaw Tinkabell). He has won multiple all-breed Bests in Show and won the Toy Group at the 1988 Melbourne Royal Show. He is one of many top winning Silky Terriers bred by Kay McGregor.

Photography by Twigg

Ronald Coolaroo out of Farmer's Twist, both from Coolaroo stock). Voska quickly finished her Swiss and international championships. Mrs. Dedie later imported two more bitches, Farmer's Laure (by Fr. and Int. Ch. Farmer's Tango out of Farmer's Ursulla), and Karen of Angel Face (by Swed., Ger., Sw., and Int. Ch. Swedehill's Gwai Billa out of Hickory's Blackeyed Susan).

Mrs. Dedie bred a top winning bitch, Fr., Lux., Mon. and Int. Ch. Mousseline St. Didier, owned by Mr. and Mrs. Guy David of France. The sire is Fr., Sw., and Int. Ch. Moore St. Didier, and the dam is Karen of Angel Face. By two years of age Mousseline had won thirty-one Bests of Breed in seven countries. In 1988 she won the Gold Medal of France and the Medal of Prestige for her wins in France and other European countries.

Italy

Two Silky Terriers—a dog and a bitch—were brought to Italy by Delia Morgotti Montanari in 1984. Both were bred by Pam Laperruque of California. The dog was Am. and Int. Ch. Centarra's Billy Th' Kid (by Tak'Ope Tu-Shu out of Centarra Sweet Tibbie Dunbar). The bitch was Centarra's Been Silver Kist (by Centarra's Chips Ahoy out of Coo Mar Centarra Blu'N Breezy). Their first litter, in 1985, produced Falpala Arcibald. In 1986 Delia imported another bitch, Centarra's Calamity Jane (by Tak'Ope Tu-Shu out of Coo-Mar's Clarique).

5

The Silky Terrier Standards

A BREED STANDARD is the written description of the ideal specimen of that breed. There has never been a dog of any breed that did not exhibit some major or minor fault. Dedicated Silky Terrier breeders strive to breed Silkys that conform as closely as possible to the Standard. The Silky Terrier sketch in this chapter serves as a good illustration of the Standard.

In 1987 the American Kennel Club asked parent clubs to rearrange their breed Standard so that all would have the same format and, wherever possible, the same terminology. The Silky Terrier Club of America was among the first to comply with this request. At the same time the Standard, which had been in effect since 1959, was clarified.

THE AMERICAN KENNEL CLUB
SILKY TERRIER STANDARD
(Adopted in 1989)

General Appearance

The Silky Terrier is a true "toy terrier." He is moderately low set, slightly longer than tall, of refined bone structure, but of sufficient substance to suggest the ability to hunt and kill domestic rodents. His coat is silky in texture, parted from the stop to the tail and presents a well groomed but not sculptured appearance. His inquisitive nature and joy of life make him an ideal companion.

Size, Proportion, Substance

Size Shoulder height from nine to ten inches. Deviation in either direction is undesirable.

Proportion The body is about one fifth longer than the dog's height at the withers.

Substance Lightly built with strong but rather fine bone.

Head

The head is strong, wedge-shaped, and moderately long. *Expression* piercingly keen, *eyes* small, dark, almond shaped with dark rims. Light eyes are a serious fault. *Ears* are small, V-shaped, set high and carried erect without any tendency to flare obliquely off the skull. *Skull* flat, and not too wide between the ears. The skull is slightly longer than the muzzle. *Stop* shallow. The *nose* is black. *Teeth* strong and well aligned, scissors bite. An undershot or overshot bite is a serious fault.

Neck, Topline and Body

The *neck* fits gracefully into sloping shoulders. It is medium long, fine, and to some degree crested. The *topline* is level. A topline showing a roach or dip is a serious fault. *Chest* medium wide and deep enough to extend down to the elbows. The *body* is moderately low set and about one fifth longer than the dog's height at the withers. The body is measured from the point of the shoulder (or

An illustration of the Silky Terrier breed Standard.   *Drawing by Pamela Powers*

forechest) to the rearmost projection of the upper thigh (or point of the buttocks). A body which is too short is a fault, as is a body which is too long. The *tail* is docked, set high and carried at twelve to two o'clock position.

Forequarters

Well laid back shoulders, together with proper angulation at the upper arm, set the forelegs nicely under the body. Forelegs are strong, straight and rather fine-boned. *Feet* small, cat-like, round, compact. Pads are thick and springy while nails are strong and dark colored. White or flesh-colored nails are a fault. The feet point straight ahead, with no turning in or out. Dewclaws, if any, are removed.

Hindquarters

Thighs well muscled and strong, but not so developed as to appear heavy. Well angulated stifles with low hocks which are parallel when viewed from behind. *Feet* as in front.

Coat

Straight, single, glossy, silky in texture. On matured specimens the coat falls below and follows the body outline. It should not approach floor length. On the top of the head, the hair is so profuse as to form a topknot, but long hair on the face and ears is objectionable. The hair is parted on the head and down over the back to the root of the tail. The tail is well coated but devoid of plume. Legs should have short hair from the pastern and hock joints to the feet. The feet should not be obscured by the leg furnishings.

Color

Blue and tan. The blue may be silver blue, pigeon blue or slate blue, the tan deep and rich. The blue extends from the base of the skull to the tip of the tail, down the forelegs to the elbows, and half way down the outside of the thighs. On the tail the blue should be very dark. Tan appears on muzzle and cheeks, around the base of the ears, on the legs and feet and around the vent. The topknot should be silver or fawn which is lighter than the tan points.

Gait

Should be free, light-footed, lively and straightforward. Hind-quarters should have strong propelling power. Toeing in or out is to be faulted.

Temperament

The keenly alert air of the terrier is characteristic, with shyness or excessive nervousness to be faulted. The manner is quick, friendly, responsive.

THE AUSTRALIAN NATIONAL KENNEL COUNCIL AUSTRALIAN SILKY TERRIER STANDARD (Amended in 1981 and reformatted in 1985)

(This Standard is also that of the Fédération Cynologique Internationale, which includes all European countries.) The Kennel Club in Great Britain has adopted a brief Standard for the breed, which they have copyrighted.

General Appearance

The dog is compact, moderately low set, of medium length with a refined structure but of sufficient substance to suggest the ability to hunt and kill domestic rodents. It should display terrier characteristics, embodying keen alertness, activity and soundness. The parted, straight silky hair presents a well-groomed appearance.

Head and Skull

Of moderate length, slightly shorter from the tip of the nose to between the eyes than from the same position to the occiput. The head must be strong and of terrier character, being moderately broad between the ears; the skull flat and without fullness between the eyes, with fine silky topknot, not falling over the eyes (a long fall of hair on the foreface or cheeks is very objectionable). Nose black.

Eyes

Should be small, round, not prominent, dark as possible in colour with a keen intelligent expression.

Ch. Lylac Blue Prince (by Lylac Playboy out of Prairie Dail), an Australian import, was a multiple STCA Specialty Best of Breed winner with six Bests in Show. He was also an Iradell Trophy winner. Bred by Nancy Glynn and owned by Marjorie and Edward Howard. *Ludwig*

Ears

Should be small, V-shaped with fine leather, set high on the skull, pricked, and entirely free from long hair.

Mouth

Strong jaws, teeth even and not cramped, the upper incisors fitting closely over the lower (scissor bite). Lips tight and clean.

Neck

Medium length, refined and slightly crested, fitting gracefully into the shoulders. Well covered with long silky hair.

Forequarters

Shoulders fine and well laid back, fitting with well angulated upper arms snugly to the ribs. Elbows turned neither in nor out. The forelegs have refined, round bone and are straight and set well under the body with no weakness in the pasterns.

Body

Should be moderately long in proportion to the height of the dog. Level topline, well sprung ribs extending back to strong loins. Chest of moderate depth and breadth. A topline showing a roach or dip is a serious fault.

Hindquarters

The thighs must be well developed and the stifles should be well turned and the hocks well bent. When viewed from behind the hocks should be well let down and parallel with each other.

Feet

Small, well padded, cat-like, with closely knit toes, the toenails must be black or very dark.

Tail

Should be docked, set on high and carried erect but not over-gay. Should be free of feathering.

Gait/Movement

The movement should be free and true without slackness at shoulders or elbows, there should be no turning in or out of the feet or pasterns. The hindquarters should have strong propelling power with ample flexibility at stifles and hocks. Viewed from behind the movement should be neither too close nor too wide.

Coat

Must be flat, fine and glossy and of a silky texture with a length of coat from 13 to 15 centimeters (5 to 6 inches) from behind the ears to the set on of the tail, but must not impede the dog's action. The legs from knees and hocks to feet free from long hair.

Colour

Blue and tan or grey-blue and tan, the richer the colour the better. Blue on the tail to be very dark. Silver blue or fawn topknot desirable. Distribution of blue and tan as follows: tan around the base of the ears, muzzle and on the sides of the cheeks; blue from the base of the skull to tip of tail, running down the forelegs to near the knees and down the thighs to the hocks; tan line showing down the stifles and from the knees and hocks to the toes and around the vent. The body colour must be free from smut or dark shading. Black colouring is permissible in puppies, blue colour must be established by 18 months of age.

Size

Height: Approximately 23 centimeters (approximately 9 inches) at the withers, bitches slightly less.

Weight: Desirable weight from 3.5 to 4.5 kilograms (approximately eight to ten pounds).

Faults

Any departure from the foregoing points should be considered a fault and the seriousness with which the fault should be regarded should be in exact proportion to its degree.

Note

Male animals should have two apparently normal testicles fully descended into the scrotum.

CANADIAN KENNEL CLUB
SILKY TERRIER STANDARD

(While the format is different, this Canadian Standard—with two exceptions—was the American Kennel Club Silky Terrier Standard until 1989. The exceptions are that the American Standard called for small eyes and did not note "on the move" concerning the fault of toeing in or out.)

General Appearance

The Silky Terrier is a lightly built, moderately low set toy dog of pronounced terrier character and spirited action.

Temperament

The keen, alert air of the terrier is characteristic, with shyness or excessive nervousness to be faulted. The manner is quick, friendly, responsive.

Size

Weight ranges from 8–10 pounds (4–5 kilograms). Shoulder height from 9–10 inches (23–25 centimeters). Pronounced diminutiveness (such as a height of less than 8 inches (20 centimeters) is not desired; it accentuates the quality of toyishness as opposed to the breed's definite terrier character.

Ch. Fawn Hill Lucknow Sweet N'Sour, a Best in Show, Specialty and Iradell Trophy winner. She won three consecutive Bests of Breed at Silky Terrier Club of America Specialty shows. She was bred by Verna Tucker. She retired the Ch. Wexford Pogo Memorial Trophy for her owners, William and Stephany Monteleone. Her sire was Ch. Rita's Firebrand of Fawnhill; her dam, Ch. Fawn Hill Sweet Rosie O'Grady.

Coat and Colour

Coat flat, in texture fine, glossy, silky; on matured specimens the desired length of coat from behind the ears to the set on of the tail is from 5–6 inches (13–15 centimeters). On the top of the head the hair is so profuse as to form a topknot, but long hair on face and ears is objectionable. Legs from knee and hock joints to feet should be free from long hair. The hair is parted on the head and down over the back to the root of the tail. Colour blue and tan. The blue may be silver blue, pigeon blue or slate blue, the tan deep and rich. The blue extends from the base of the skull to the tip of the tail, down the forelegs to the pasterns, and down the thighs to the hocks. On the tail the blue should be very dark. Tan appears on the muzzle and cheeks, around the base of the ears, below the pasterns and hocks, and around the vent. There is a tan spot over each eye. The topknot should be silver or fawn.

Head

The head is strong, wedge-shaped, and moderately long. The skull is a trifle longer than the muzzle, in proportion about three-fifths for the skull, two-fifths for the muzzle. Skull flat, and not too wide between the ears. Stop shallow. The nose is black. Teeth strong and well aligned. Scissors bite. Eyes dark in colour and piercingly keen in expression. Ears small, V-shaped and pricked. They are set high and carried erect without any tendency to flare obliquely off the skull.

Neck

The neck fits gracefully into sloping shoulders. It is medium long, fine and to some degree crested along its topline.

Forequarters

Well laid back shoulders, together with good angulation at the upper arm, set the forelegs nicely under the body. Forelegs are strong, straight, and rather fine boned.

Body

Low-set, about one fifth longer than the dog's height at the withers. The backline is straight, with a just perceptible rounding over the loins. Brisket medium wide, and deep enough to extend down to the elbows.

Hindquarters

Thighs well muscled and strong, but not so developed as to appear heavy. Legs moderately angulated at the stifles and hocks, with the hocks low and equidistant from the hock joints to the ground. Feet small, cat-like, round, compact. Pads are thick and springy while the nails are strong and dark coloured. The feet point straight ahead, with no turning in or out. Dewclaws, if any, are removed.

Tail

The tail is set high and carried erect or semi-erect but not over gay. It is docked and well coated but devoid of plume.

Gait

Should be free, light footed, lively and straight forward. Hindquarters should have strong propelling power.

Faults

Shyness or excessive nervousness. A bite markedly undershot or overshot is a serious fault. Light eyes are a fault. A too-short body is a fault. White or flesh-coloured nails are a fault. Toeing in or out on the move is to be faulted.

6

Discussion of the Silky Terrier Standard

FOR MORE THAN THIRTY YEARS Silky Terriers were judged according to the specifications set forth in the breed Standard compiled by the American Kennel Club in 1959. It was the same as the current Standard for the breed in Canada, quoted in Chapter 5, with the exceptions noted there.

With recognition of the breed the Silky Terrier Club of America became the parent club for the breed in this country. As such the club is responsible for devising the breed Standard. Breed Standards can be changed only by a majority vote of the parent club's membership. The Standard must then be approved by the AKC.

Since 1959 two committees appointed by the club have reviewed the Standard. Both were dissolved without making any recommendations for changes. Each time they saw a need for clarification, but arrived at a stalemate. The primary contention was whether to introduce a disqualification for Silkys over ten pounds in weight. Such a disqualification would have resulted in eliminating numerous Silkys that have contributed much to the breed.

At the request of the AKC the Standard was reformatted in 1989. At that time some long overdue clarifications and changes were made.

The newly adopted Standard retains the same height specifications but eliminates any mention of weight. The Standard specifies a shoulder height from nine to ten inches and adds that a deviation in either direction is undesirable. A Silky Terrier's weight depends entirely on the size of his bone, which should be strong but rather fine, and his muscular development. His body should feel solid and sturdy, not fragile.

The Standard's general description of the breed aptly portrays the Silky as a true toy terrier. Emphasis should be placed on the word "terrier."

The moderately long head, with the skull just slightly longer than the muzzle, imparts a terrier, rather than a toyish, appearance. The foreface should be strong, with sufficient space for uncrowded teeth.

A weak muzzle is nearly always accompanied by missing or crowded incisors. The teeth should meet in a scissors bite, which means that the outer surfaces of the lower incisor teeth engage with the inner surfaces of the upper incisors when the mouth is shut. Undershot and overshot bites are serious faults. An overshot bite occurs when the lower incisors are situated some distance behind their upper counterparts. An undershot bite occurs when the lower incisors are situated in front of those in the upper jaw.

Small, dark, almond-shaped eyes give Silkys their alert, intelligent terrier expression. Round eyes are usually large and result in a soulful look, which is not typical of the breed's character. Light eye rims are as serious a fault as light eyes and are usually accompanied by a light nose and toenails. These are indications of pigment deterioration.

It is extremely important that the ears are high set, small and V-shaped. They should point straight up. The keen terrier expression is lost when ears flare to the sides of the head or are rounded at the tips.

A slightly crested neck of medium length is essential for proud head carriage. A long neck will not be in balance with the body. A short neck, the result of straight shoulders, gives a Silky a cloddy appearance.

An illustration of the head as described in the Standard: "strong, wedge-shaped, and moderately long. . . . The skull is slightly longer than the muzzle. Stop shallow." Illustrated by Ch. Redway Splinters (by Ch. Wexford Pogo out of Brenhill Splinters), bred and owned by Peggy Smith.

An illustration of correct ears: "small, V-shaped, set high and carried erect." Illustrated by Ch. Larkspurs Blue Chip (by Silti's Joy Boy out of Ch. Ronco's Skat Dancer), bred and owned by Carolyn and James Stewart.

The moderately low set body, about one fifth longer than the height at the withers, gives an eye-pleasing balance. These are the identical body proportions of the previous standard; however, that standard did not specify how the body should be measured. One author incorrectly stated that a Silky Terrier that was ten inches at the shoulder should measure twelve inches from the shoulder to the tail. This, of course, would make the backline one fifth longer and would result in a long-bodied dog. The Silky Terrier's body should not be long; neither should it be short. The Standard requires the same compact, medium-length dog as described in the Australian Standard for the breed.

Tail carriage is an excellent indication of proper and improper temperament. An outgoing Silky Terrier, with the correct high-set tail, will carry his tail from a twelve to two o'clock position. A Silky will sometimes drop his tail slightly when he is standing relaxed. However, his tail should move into the proper position when he begins gaiting. Some Silkys, when excited, will carry their tails over their backs. This should be a temporary position. If this appears to be the permanent tail carriage it should be considered a minor fault. However, this is much preferred to a tail carried below the two o'clock position. A correctly set tail that is carried low indicates a lack of terrier temperament.

The forelegs should be parallel. They should be set back, well under the body. This requires good angulation of the shoulders and upper arms. When they are not well angulated, movement is restricted and the legs are set forward with little or no chest in front of the legs.

Backs that are not level continue to be a major fault. This can be partially blamed on the previous Standard, which led some to believe that a roached topline was correct. The present Standard, which notes a roach or dip as a serious fault, should result in improvement in this area.

Sufficient exercise is essential for the required well-muscled thighs. The standard calls for low hocks, which requires the rear pasterns to be short, not long. These requirements are often ignored.

The correct Silky Terrier coat is adequately described in the Standard: straight, single, glossy and silky in texture. No allowance is made for woolly or harsh coats. Harsh coats are rare, but those with a woolly texture are frequently seen in the show ring—some even winning their championship titles. These woolly coats are most often seen on dogs that will remain black at maturity. Body coats that approach floor length are a fault, not a virtue.

These parted coats clearly show the dark roots that are necessary for a coat to be silver *blue*. An incorrect silver coat, without blue, will be the same color at the roots. On the left is Brenhill Splinters, on the right is her daughter, Ch. Redway Splinters.

The dog on the left has correct parallel legs; the dog on the right has badly bowed legs and its ears are too large, rounded and flare to the side.

Illustrating the "small, cat-like, round, compact" feet described in the breed Standard is two-month-old future Ch. Redway Buster (by Ch. Wexford Pogo out of his daughter Redway Smith's Gamble), bred by Peggy Smith and owned by Beverly Lehnig.

Coat color is often misinterpreted. The Standard describes the body coat color of mature Silkys. It should be silver blue, pigeon blue or slate blue—never black. Black puppy coats should change to blue as they mature. The standard calls for the tan to be deep and rich. It does not specify that the blue should be deep and rich. Many judges seem to think that only the darker blues are correct. The silver blue color is equally correct and can be striking when accompanied by rich tan points. A silver blue coat must be dark at the roots, which are easily seen where the coat is parted on the back. A silver coat, without dark roots, is not silver blue and is an unacceptable color.

The black hairs on the face and around the eyes, called a black mask, should grow out by the time the puppy reaches six months of age. If it does not, the face and topknot will probably have an undesirable sooty appearance at maturity instead of clear color.

A properly constructed Silky Terrier's gait will be effortless.

The breed's temperament is described well in the Standard.

THE SILKY THROUGH THE YEARS

Mrs. C. Bede Maxwell, a well-known Australian author, lecturer, canine journalist and dog show judge, made the United States her home in 1955. Soon after her arrival she began to champion the cause of Silky Terriers in numerous dog publications.

Maxie, as she is known to her friends, is a lady of many talents and interests. She was the author of three books, on widely diverse subjects, published in Australia. Two books by her have been published in this country, both by Howell Book House. *The New German Shorthaired Pointer,* in its fourth printing, is considered, worldwide, to be the definitive book on the breed. *The Truth About Sporting Dogs* is a veritable gold mine on the true history of the gundog breeds.

Mrs. Maxwell judged the first Silky Terrier Club of America's Sanctioned Match. Her choice for Best in Match was Rinaldo Navarro's Maurie Lady Rita (by Ch. Wexford Pogo out of Mitry Lady Mandy). Best Opposite Sex in Match was Frances Van Etten's imported Bowenvale Blue Boy (by Aus. Ch. Bo Bo out of Dainty Girl). Both soon became champions.

The following is her critique of the Match:

The Silky Terrier Club of America's exciting, historical first Sanctioned Match was held on August 13, 1960. No hitch marred the well

Correct | Muzzle too short | Muzzle too long

Head proportions.

Correct | Set wide, large and flaring to the side

Too large and rounded

Ear sets.

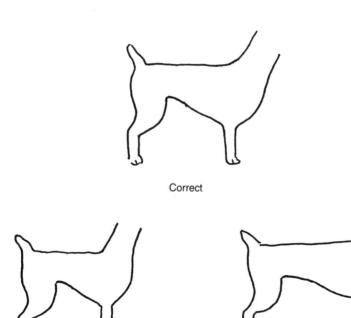

Correct

Body too short

Body too long

Body proportions.

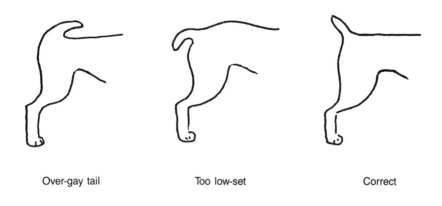

Over-gay tail

Too low-set

Correct

Tail sets.

 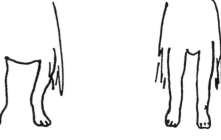

Correct	Fiddle front	Narrow front

Front assembly.

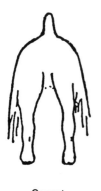  

Correct	Cowhocked	Narrow rear

Rear assembly.

Splay foot	Cat foot

Feet.

organized proceedings and a big entry rewarded the Show Committee for hard work and the best muster seen out so far in this country.

Variation in type, however, was sufficient to permit breed students to estimate trends, an important matter in a breed so widely dispersed as to make it very difficult for Silky breeders across the nation to use that most valuable of tools available to any breeder—that of comparison.

It will remain a constant pride that the Committee honored me with the judge's ribbon and my further pride as an Aussie is that I am able to report to Silky owners far and wide that the entry established beyond any hope I had dared to entertain that these American breeders know where they are heading—and why. Give or take a loved pet or two, the 23 dogs competing were all striving towards the ideal as the standard expresses. Not that they lacked faults—Oh, goodness me, no. All dogs, all breeds, have faults. But, what was more important, they also possessed virtues, and those are the important factors, the virtues.

Firmly, it is my belief—not only mine!—that in judging dogs it is much more important to assess virtues than to find faults. Blind Freddie can see faults but virtues seem to escape even those at ringside with more eyes than Argus. *These are the folk who pounce on needles and miss haystacks.*

So, first to the virtues of the Silkys I saw at Los Altos Hills. In a majority of dogs size and type were as one would wish, a few too big, a few too small, but the majority firmly shelved within the required weight and height bracketings. That type was recognizable is, after all, the most important thing in any breed. As a great English all-rounder has written "First requirement in judging is that a dog should look like the breed it is supposed to be." That has not always at all times been true of Silkys from which I have averted somewhat pained eyes, but it *was* true of the majority of dogs I saw here. Good or not so good, they were in the main *Silkys.* And that of itself, after the difficult times through which breeders have been groping, is very important and a great gain.

Heads? It seems to me that heads in the breed could be the least of the breeders' worries. A few somewhat overlong in muzzle, a poppy eye or so, but otherwise good as to proportion. Ears were another story, I saw floppy, bat-wing, list-to-port, list-to-starboard, all undesirable and ruining the alert and perky expression that characterises the breed at its best. Breeders, write that in the little black book—*ears to be taken into careful consideration.* Mouths, apart from here and there a veteran that had come off second best in the battle with a vet's forceps, were for the most part extremely good. Nice firm white bites correctly positioned.

Length in relation to height—for the most part good. Outline not always as desirable, level backs not everywhere in evidence and this quite often related to underpinnings. On this breeders will have to confer—take a stand in relation to the front and rear assemblies of their dogs. I saw out-elbows, bulldog fronts (over wide) and, what seemed to me much, much worse, some dogs with foreleg bones bent like Pekingese. Not so long ago a new Silky owner who had bought three to start a kennel, on discerning that all three new acquisitions were "bowlegged as cowboys" felt sure there was something wrong with the compilation of the standard that required straight front legs in the Silky Terrier. NO lady, NO—let's have none of the bent front, ever. Nor is it universal as those three seemed to suggest, but merely a misfortune to be eventually corrected in the breed. I saw too many poor fronts but, at the same time, I saw a gratifying number of good ones, sufficient to make it clear that not *all* Silkys are "bowlegged as cowboys." Good fronts, by the way, in several cases influenced my placings.

Hindquarters must also be assessed with care, many up-sloping toplines come from insufficiently angulated stifles and overlong hocks; a combination that also plagues Dachshund breeders. Yet dogs with correct angulation and hocks correct for breed size were in the entry and these would have something useful to contribute to the breed. Feet too should be a matter for breeders' concern. By and large it was impossible to find any feet that, to my mind, matched with the standard requirement for "cat feet." What I saw were mostly out-turned, rather flat, thin padded feet with, in the bitches especially, over-long toe nails that needed cutting.

Color. Mostly good, and in the top dogs very good, especially when the champions appeared. However, there was a percentage of undesirables in respect of this important characteristic of the breed, notably blacks, whites (which is my interpretation of an all-silver dog) and those with gold in their body blue. There seems to be some uncertainly as to what is actually meant by "blue" for a Silky. Wide latitude is permitted from silver *blue* (light) through slate *blue* (dark). The majority of Silkys that were shown fitted into this range.

Final thought; remembering all those nice little dogs and estimating the improvement they represent over what has been brought out in the past, it is still true, as I have elsewhere observed, that Silky breeders must walk their tightrope, falling neither to Yorkshire nor Australian Terrier side. I penalized some dogs for being "too Yorkie" type. It could be a dangerous trap for Silky breeders to lean toward Yorkie type. *It is less than wise for breeders to attempt to challenge him for length of coat!* The Silky brings other wares to market; his own individual characteristics. He is, or should be, an entirely different dog as the standard requires him to be. He is *not,* as unkind critics have described him, a smudged carbon of a Yorkie. The Silky is no smudged carbon. He is to his own pattern.

Much of Mrs. Maxwell's advice still applies today. She noted a few Silkys with somewhat overlong muzzles. This fault is rarely seen today. Instead we often see Silky Terriers with muzzles that are too short. The dogs entered in that Match were either imports or their close descendants. They were bred according to the Australian Standard's correct head proportions specifying that the skull is slightly longer than the muzzle.

Head proportions are no longer the least of the breeders' worries. Silkys with short muzzles tend to be Yorkshire Terrier type in head. The 1989 American Standard has been corrected to agree with the head proportions of the Australian Standard, and this change should result in considerable improvement in this area.

Another trait tending toward Yorkshire Terrier type is the excessively long coat. The 1989 Standard makes coat length clear by stating: "On matured specimens the coat falls below and follows the body outline. It should not approach floor length." Thus, extreme length of coat is a fault, not a virtue.

Mrs. Maxwell's comment—"ears to be taken into careful consideration"—is as important today as it was then. For the correct alert, perky, and typical Silky expression ears *must* be, as described in the Standard, "small, V-shaped, set high and carried erect without any tendency to flare obliquely off the skull." Such ears are rare. Many are still set too far apart and pointing east and west. The tips of the ears should point straight up.

Most Silkys have the proper scissors bite and well-aligned teeth. However, faults have crept in and are being perpetuated. Judges as well as breeders can be blamed for this. Until a few years ago Silky Terriers had some of the best dentition to be seen in the toy breeds. Many judges think dentition is unimportant in toy dogs. These are usually the same judges who think soundness is also unimportant in Toys. Both *are* important. Few overshot or undershot bites are seen in the show ring, but judges and breeders should be sure that all six upper and lower incisors are present. Missing incisors indicate weak, snipy muzzles. Missing premolars are also a fault, although not as severe a fault as missing incisors.

Length of body in relation to height is generally correct, and the 1989 Standard dispels any confusion as to how this should be measured. It states: "The body is measured from the point of the shoulder (or forechest) to the rearmost projection of the upper thigh (or point of the buttocks)."

A major fault continues to be toplines that are not level. The previous Standard, which referred to the "backline" being straight, contained the phrase "with a just perceptible rounding over the loins." This led some judges to believe that a topline that was not level was correct. The new Standard should help to eliminate this fault because it states: "The topline is level. A topline showing a roach or dip is a serious fault."

Mrs. Maxwell noted that the Silky Terrier's feet should be a matter for breeders' attention. This has become a matter of serious concern; now the cat-like feet described in the Standard are seldom seen.

Calling attention to present-day faults does not mean that the breed hasn't improved since those early days. Far from it! It has made tremendous progress. Many fine Silky Terriers have garnered countless awards at Specialties, in the Groups, and in Best in Show competition.

7

Comparison of the Silky, Yorkshire and Australian Terrier Breeds

THOSE WHO ARE unfamiliar with these breeds often mistake a Silky Terrier for a Yorkshire Terrier or an Australian Terrier. At American Kennel Club shows the Silky Terrier and the Yorkshire Terrier are exhibited in the Toy Group; the Australian Terrier is in the Terrier Group. The three breeds are distinctly different.

There is considerable difference in the size of these breeds. The Australian Terrier is ten to eleven inches at the withers and *long* in proportion to the height of the dog. The Silky Terrier's shoulder height is nine to ten inches, and his body is *slightly longer* than his height. The Yorkshire Terrier has fine bone, his weight must not exceed seven pounds and he has a rather *short back*. The Yorkshire

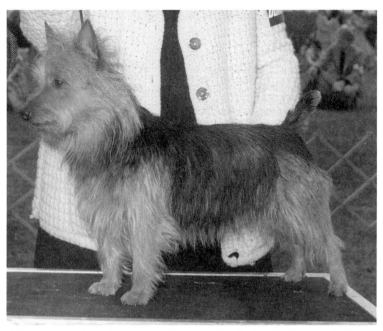

A fine example of a typical blue and tan Australian Terrier, Ch. Regency April Lady, bred by Ida Ellen Weinstock and Jerry McCulley, owned by Ida Ellen and Ruth Weinstock.

The top winning Yorkshire Terrier of all time, Ch. Cede Higgins, bred by C. D. Lawrence, owned by Barbara and Charles Switzer, and handled by their daughter Marlene Lutovsky. *Carl Lindemaier*

Terrier is much smaller than the Australian or Silky Terrier. The preferred weight of a show-ring Yorkie is four to five pounds. The Australian Terrier, because of his medium bone and longer body, is noticeably larger than the shorter-bodied, rather fine-boned Silky Terrier.

The Australian and Silky Terrier's heads, other than size and furnishings, are quite similar. The Australian Terrier's muzzle, which is equal to the length of the skull, is slightly longer than that of the Silky Terrier. The Australian Terrier's topknot is not as profuse as that of the Silky Terrier and is not parted. Neither breed should have long hair on the muzzle. By contrast, the fall of hair on the Yorkshire Terrier's head is so long that it is tied up with bows and the hair on the muzzle is very long. The Yorkshire Terrier head is small with "the muzzle not too long."

The coat texture of the Silky Terrier and Yorkshire Terrier are similar, with both breed Standards requiring it to be glossy and silky. Theirs is a single coat. The Yorkshire Terrier's show-ring coat reaches the ground. The Silky Terrier's coat, although long, should not reach this length but should fall below and follow the outline of the body. The Australian Terrier's harsh body coat is only two and one-half inches long, with a soft undercoat, making it a double coat.

The color of the Australian Terrier can be blue and tan, solid sandy or solid red. The Yorkshire Terrier is blue and tan, with the body blue a dark steel color and the headfall a rich golden tan. The Silky Terrier is also blue and tan; however, the body blue of the Silky Terrier can range from silver blue to slate blue, and the Silky's topknot is light in color, either fawn or silver.

The three breeds should be easily identified by keeping these marked differences in mind.

Ch. Silti's Superstition (by Ch. Silti Tumbleweed Pete out of Ch. Silti's Pego My Heart). Bred and owned by Mary T. Estrin.

8

The Character of the Silky Terrier

MUCH HAS BEEN WRITTEN regarding the character of all breeds, large and small. Many breed characteristics are inherent, but some, as happens with people, are formed by their environment.

Whatever we contribute toward the development of intelligence and character is of enormous importance and well worth the effort. A dull child is one who has probably not been exposed to reasonable socialization. This too is true of dogs.

Silky Terriers want and need socialization and discipline. No two are completely alike. Each is an individual even when raised by the same people.

The Silky Terrier is small—but only in stature. Size is of little importance to a Silky. The brave, proud and dignified attitude reveals all the characteristics of a terrier.

Silky Terriers live to please and are quick to respond to commands when they understand them. Their ability to concentrate for lengthy periods of time makes them easy to teach and fun to work with.

Millburn Brandywine, as a puppy, with his fourteen-year-old Miniature Smooth Dachshund buddy. He was bred by Jane Powell and owned by Virginia Branham.

He really *does* climb trees! Starview's Mighty Micajah, bred and owned by Dick and Jerry Titley.

Future Ch. Silti Tumbleweed Pete, at four months of age (by Ch. Redway For Pete's Sake out of Ch. Silti's Dame Ditto), bred by Mary T. Estrin and co-owned with Peggy Smith. Pete is still enjoying life at sixteen years of age.

Silky Terriers are polite and happy to see visitors arrive, but they leave little doubt as to where their real affection lies. They are happiest when they have their masters' undivided attention and they thrive on this companionship.

They are devoted to their families, including the children. However, as with all small dogs, it is best to introduce Silkys to children when the dogs are puppies.

They are naturally clean little dogs. They enjoy the everyday care and attention from their families but reserve the right to choose who will be their best friend.

9

Choosing a Silky Terrier Puppy

CHOOSING A PUPPY is an important decision that should not be made in haste. Nearly all puppies are appealing, but impulse buying should be avoided.

It is important that all members of the family should want the pup. Don't depend upon the child who promises to feed, water, exercise, groom and train the puppy. His or her enthusiasm may soon wane. These responsibilities should be left to an adult.

For a number of reasons it's best to buy your puppy from a breeder. You will have the breeder's experience in helping you to pick the puppy that seems best suited to your requirements. You will be able to see the puppy's dam, evaluate her temperament and have some indication of how your puppy will mature. It may not be possible to see the puppy's sire, as he may be owned by someone who lives some distance away. However, the breeder will undoubtedly have his picture to show you.

Show quality is impossible to accurately determine in a young puppy. Experienced, reputable breeders won't sell young puppies as show prospects. If you're seeking a Silky Terrier for the show ring it's wise to buy an older pup or a young dog.

Two-day-old puppies, with undocked tails, and their dam, Ch. Silky Acres Redway Meredith, bred and owned by Patricia Walton and Peggy Smith.

Tail docking and removal of dewclaws should be done at five or six days of age rather than the often-recommended three or four days. Tails will usually be the correct length when they are docked just past the tan on the underside of the tail, leaving about one-eighth inch of the black portion.

Ch. Weeblu's Windsong of Joy, CD, with her litter after tail docking. She was bred by Florence Males and owned with Peggy Lawson.

118

Seven is an unusually large litter. The average litter is three or four. This six-week-old litter was sired by Ch. Wexford Pogo when he was over fourteen years of age. The dam was Canberra Cupie, owned by Dorothy and Karen Vanderhoof.

Future Ch. Alcamar's Dancin' Duchess (by Ch. Kiku's Luv Bug of Vamaro out of Ch. Alcamar's Silver Dollar Dolly), owned by Marilyn and Raymond Mishoe and bred by Irma Marshall and Janet Aslett. Pictured at three months with one ear pricked.

Pictured one month later with her well-set ears, which have not yet been plucked.

From puppy to veteran. Pictured at fifteen weeks of age is future Group-winning Ch. Rebel Dandy Andy (by Ch. Redway Buster out of Rebel April Angel), bred by Beverly Lehnig and owned by Patricia Walton.

Andy at sixteen months of age.

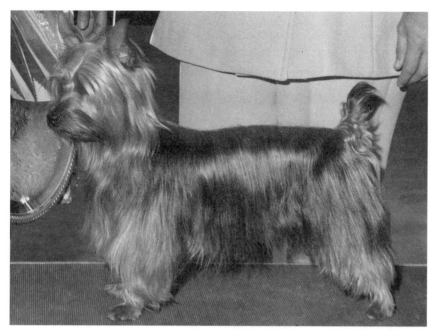

At two years, winning Group 1.

At thirteen years, winning the Veteran Dog class at a Silky Terrier Club of America Specialty show.

Before contacting any breeders, you should first do some homework. Carefully study the structural requirements of the breed Standard and the chapter that discusses it in detail. Also read the chapters on grooming, care and character.

Silky Terrier puppies should be interested in everything around them and responsive to people. They should not be timid. Temperament is of primary importance whether you are purchasing a Silky as a pet or to show.

It is not possible to determine all of the breed Standard's requirements in a puppy. Young puppies' eyes, which appear to be dark, may become light as they mature. This inclination can sometimes be seen in bright daylight. Mouths that will become over- or undershot can usually be detected in young puppies, but dentition cannot be fully determined until the permanent teeth come in. Teething usually begins at about four months. Puppies' ears, which have been erect, may drop to a pendent position while they are teething.

Some Silky puppies are born with some white on their chests. If it is barely discernible when the puppy is two months of age it will probably disappear. However, if it appears as a large patch at this age it will undoubtedly remain.

If the puppy's front legs are bowed they will not improve with age. Rear legs that appear to be cow hocked may improve with muscle development. Puppies' backlines should be straight, although they may not always be level. Their fronts and rears often do not grow at the same rate.

It is interesting to note that the majority of Silky Terrier breeders and exhibitors purchased their first Silky as a pet, with no intention of becoming dog show exhibitors. When they decided to enter the world of dog shows, some were fortunate enough to have obtained Silkys with sufficient virtues to warrant exhibiting them. Others proceeded to purchase their second Silky, this time of show quality. For this reason you may want to consider buying the best puppy you can afford. At two to three months of age those puppies that appear promising will probably be priced only slightly higher than those that may already exhibit minor or major faults.

The Silky Terrier Club of America publishes the annual *Member Breeder List,* which is available on request. The address of the current club secretary can be obtained from the American Kennel Club, 51 Madison Avenue, New York, NY 10010.

10

Caring for
a Silky Terrier

WHILE SILKY TERRIERS are classified as a Toy breed, they are not fragile. They are sturdy little terriers.

Preparations for training your puppy should begin with the purchase of a dog crate before bringing the dog home. Lightweight, easy-to-clean plastic crates are available through most dog supply shops or catalogs.

There are many advantages and no disadvantages to using a crate. When a dog is introduced to a crate at an early age, it will regard it as a welcome haven and, if the door is left open, will probably enter it often for a peaceful nap.

To indoctrinate your Silky to its crate, put the puppy in for short periods of time at first, with a toy to chew on or a dog biscuit. Praise him when he remains there quietly. Never put a Silky in his crate as a reprimand.

Using a crate will facilitate housebreaking the puppy. Silkys are clean dogs and do not like to soil their beds. It should be closed in its crate during the night and taken outside directly from the crate in the morning. Take the pup outside frequently during the day and

Pictured at eleven months of age, enjoying a Colorado winter, is future Ch. Tru Blu Bei Under My Spell, UD, bred by Linda Mowrer and owned by her and Linda Hart.

always praise it when it cooperates. If a regular schedule is maintained, the pup will soon be housebroken.

Dogs are much safer in vehicles if they are closed in their crates rather than allowed to ride loose. A crate can prevent injury that could result from a sudden stop and can keep a dog from being thrown from the car in an accident.

Puppies need and love to chew, especially when they are teething. Give them an assortment of safe chew toys. They cannot distinguish between their toys and your belongings if you are not there to correct them. Crating will eliminate unwanted chewing when you are away.

Do not let your Silky become a finicky eater. This is usually the result of feeding him food intended for humans. For proper nutrition use one of the many quality foods made especially for dogs.

A regular schedule of inoculations against diseases and boosters should be maintained according to your veterinarian's advice.

Consult your veterinarian if you suspect your Silky has worms. If worming is necessary he or she will provide you with safe medication to eliminate them. The presence of worms is sometimes suspected when the problem is actually a heavy secretion in the dog's anal glands. This is simple to rectify, and your veterinarian can show you how to take care of it yourself.

Heartworm infestation can be fatal. If they are prevalent where you live or where you may be visiting with your Silky, your veterinarian will prescribe a preventative medicine. The instructed dosage should be faithfully adhered to.

It is extremely important to keep your Silky's teeth clean to avoid a buildup of tartar, which causes loss of teeth and health problems. Your veterinarian can instruct you on proper home cleaning and may recommend a product to retard the accumulation of tartar. Your Silky's teeth should be inspected regularly, such as when he receives his booster shots. Have his teeth professionally cleaned if the condition warrants it.

Ear care is also important. The insides of the ears should be cleaned regularly with a small amount of alcohol on cotton balls. Be extremely careful if it is necessary to use cotton swabs to remove an accumulation of wax. Ear drums can be damaged if you probe deeply.

If you find fleas on your Silky, act promptly to avoid a heavy infestation. If this occurs, the dog's entire environment will have to be treated, not only the dog. Labels on some products warn that they

A group of friends owned by Patricia Walton. In the rear, left to right, are Ch. Rebel Dandy Andy, Ch. Redway Tomales Tom and Little Snooki. In front are Rebel September Sweetheart and Ch. Silky Acres Tiny Toby.

This eight-week-old litter shows the desirable "lift" of the ears that indicates they will become erect. Bred by Norma Baugh. They are sired by Ch. Amron's Junior Mint Bear out of Ch. Luxa's Punkin' Patch of Amron.

126

A family of Silky Terriers. On the left is Ch. Skylark's Murph the Surf; third from left is Ch. Dariuswood's Sweet Jenny Girl. Pictured with their litter, Southwind's Salty of Tweedale, Southwind's Marty O'Dariuswood, and Southwind's Are You My Molly, bred and owned by Donna Wright. Murph the Surf was bred by Madeline Meggitt and is owned by Robert Wright and Eleanor Norton.

An all-champion litter of six (by Ch. Rosewell's Blue Sounder out of Ch. Rosewell's Pollae of Baby Doe). *Left to right:* Rosewell's My Blue Shadow, Rosewell's Blue Velvet, Rosewell's Blue Blazes, Rosewell's Blue Tinker, Rosewell's Blue Boy, and Rosewell's Blue Moon. They were bred by Louise Rosewell and Myrtle Turnage and owned by Louise Rosewell. Shadow was a Group and All Toy Breeds Best in Show winner.

should not be used on puppies. Use caution if you are using more than one product at the same time. Ask your veterinarian to recommend safe products.

Have your female Silky spayed if you don't plan to breed her. This will eliminate the inconvenience of her twice-yearly heat cycles, unplanned breedings and the possibility of mammary tumors.

If you are considering breeding your Silky at some future time, your first step should be to obtain a copy of *The Joy of Breeding Your Own Show Dog,* by Anne Seranne, published by Howell Book House. This is an encyclopedia of dog breeding that will answer any questions you may have and help you avoid some of the pitfalls that are frequently experienced by novice breeders.

11

Grooming the
Silky Terrier

COMPARED WITH MANY of the long-coated breeds, Silky Terriers require a minimum amount of grooming. First and foremost, a regular schedule should be adhered to. Your Silky Terrier will enjoy the attention it receives during these sessions if it learns at an early age that grooming is a pleasant experience.

Grooming equipment is available at most pet shops, dog shows and through dog supply catalogs. Whether your Silky is a showdog or pet, there are some basic items that are required for proper grooming. You will need a natural bristle brush, a cushioned pin brush for fine hair, a comb with both narrow and wide teeth, toenail clippers, scissors and a blow dryer.

Many quality dog shampoos are available. It may be necessary to experiment with different brands to find which is best suited to your dog's coat texture. Never use shampoos intended for human hair, as they are not formulated in the proper balance for a canine coat.

If you plan to exhibit your Silky at dog shows, there are additional items you will undoubtedly want, such as thinning shears and stripping knives. Many specialty items, and a variety of shampoos, can be found only at dog shows or from dog supply catalogs.

The most convenient and satisfactory way to groom your Silky is to stand him on a table. Special grooming tables of various heights can be purchased. Many people use any small table or even the top of a washer or dryer covered with a nonslip mat.

GROOMING THE PUPPY

Puppies should be introduced to being brushed as early as six to eight weeks of age so that they can become accustomed to handling and grooming. At this age they are easily bored, so the initial sessions should be short and pleasant.

Puppies can have their first bath, if necessary, at this age. Care must be taken to prevent the puppy from becoming chilled. Puppies, as well as mature Silkys, can be conveniently bathed in a sink. Be sure to talk soothingly to the puppy, as the first bath can be a startling experience.

Wet the puppy's body coat thoroughly with warm water. Gently lather the shampoo into the coat, taking care to keep it out of the eyes. The shampoo must be thoroughly rinsed out of the coat. A spray attachment on the faucet is especially good for this. Once this is complete, wrap the puppy in a towel and blot the excess moisture from the coat.

While some owners prefer to brush their Silkys to dry the coat, most prefer to use a blow dryer. It should be used on a warm, rather than hot setting. Continue to talk soothingly to the puppy when introducing the dryer, as it may not like the noise.

Puppies require some trimming. The toenails should be trimmed frequently. Cuticle scissors or nail clippers designed for humans are sometimes easier to use than clippers designed for adult dogs.

There are often short hairs at the inside corners of the eyes that scratch against the eye and cause irritation. They can be plucked by hand or carefully trimmed with blunt-tipped scissors. In this case "plucking" does not mean pulling the hair out by the roots; it means breaking the hair off.

Hand plucking is done with the thumb and forefinger. A small amount of precipitated chalk rubbed on these fingers provides a better grip of the hair. This powder can be obtained at pharmacies.

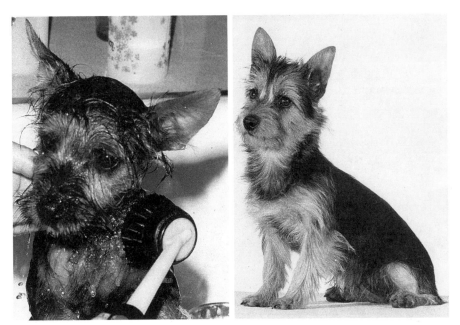

The bath . . . and the result. The puppy is future Ch. Weeblu's Princess Powder Puff, CD (by Ch. Silti's Joy Boy out of Ch. Silkallure Wee One), bred by Florence Males and owned with Peggy Lawson.

A well-groomed pair of Silky Terriers. On the left is Ch. Khara's Gotcha' Spellbound and his sister, Ch. Khara's Watch My Magic (by Ch. Roy-Dee's Big Chief Tundr' out of Tru Blu You Do That Voodoo, CD), bred and owned by Linda Hart.

Illustrating ears that have not been plucked is Sangate Earl Jocko, circa 1956 (by Redway Splinters' Boy out of Greenhills Lady Moppet), owned by Thomas Fromm and bred by Robert Garrett.

Pluck only one or two hairs at a time to avoid causing discomfort to the dog.

Long hair on the ears can be plucked by hand or trimmed with thinning shears. Although this is debatable, some fanciers believe that a heavy growth of hair on the ears can keep them from becoming erect.

The hair between the pads of the feet should be carefully trimmed with scissors. Long hair that extends past the outline of the feet can also be trimmed with scissors.

The breed Standard calls for the hair to be parted on the head and down the back to the root of the tail. It is difficult to keep a part in the short hair of a young puppy. You can begin training the part to stay in by wetting your hands with water or with a small amount of setting gel, placing them on both sides of the part, and then moving them down the sides of the puppy. As the coat lengthens the part will begin to stay in.

Silky puppies have coats of different textures. Some have a soft, fluffy puppy coat. These coats will often mat close to the skin where the mats are not readily visible. Such coats should be combed frequently to prevent mat formation. If mats occur, saturating them with water, or products available for this purpose, will facilitate their removal. Gently pull the mat apart with your fingers. The adult coat is not usually as soft textured and does not mat as easily.

Reward the puppy with special treats at the end of the grooming sessions. Frequent, short sessions will result in a puppy that is not afraid of being handled. The attention it receives will make it more comfortable when being examined by a veterinarian or dog show judge.

GROOMING THE SILKY TERRIER FOR THE SHOW RING

If you have purchased a Silky Terrier with show potential, you will need to learn a few grooming techniques to have it looking its best in the show ring. Many tips can be learned from experienced Silky Terrier exhibitors.

Ideally, the Silky Terrier is a clean-pointed breed. Such dogs require little trimming or plucking of the ears and feet. Those Silkys that are not clean pointed should be groomed to look as natural as possible without producing a sculptured appearance.

Illustrating a properly groomed topknot is Ch. Don-Els Look of Elegance (by Ch. Silkallure Casanova out of Princess Parizade), bred by Mona Bracco and owned by Don and Helen Thompson.

Whether to bathe the Silky Terrier before or after grooming is a matter of individual preference. If the dog's coat is dirty or snarled it is best to groom after the bath. There is less breakage of the hair if the mats or snarls are worked out of a wet coat. This procedure was previously described in the instructions for bathing the puppy. You may need to experiment with different shampoos to determine which is most suitable for your dog. This may also be necessary if you choose to use a creme rinse or coat conditioner. Some products will affect coat color. The American Kennel Club has strict rules that prohibit any alteration of the dog's color.

Before bathing your Silky place cotton in the ears to prevent water and shampoo from getting into them. Care should also be taken not to get shampoo in the eyes. With your Silky standing in the sink or tub, wet the coat thoroughly with warm water. Work the shampoo gently into the coat from behind the ears to the tail and down to the feet. The muzzle and topknot can usually be cleaned with a damp cloth. *Thoroughly* rinse all traces of shampoo from the coat. If you have chosen to use a creme rinse or coat conditioner, follow the instructions that are given on the product. Wrap the dog in a thick towel and gently blot, *do not rub,* the excess water from the coat.

To prevent waves in the coat and possible chilling, you will probably want to use a blow dryer rather than brush the coat to dry it. Brush the coat from the part downward, lifting the hair away from the dog's body to avoid waving. Use a warm, not hot, setting on the dryer, as a hot setting is uncomfortable for the dog and can dry out his skin and coat. You should be able to gauge how hot it is for the dog by placing your hand a few inches from the dryer. If it is too hot for you it is too hot for the dog.

When drying the topknot brush it back toward the body rather than to each side of the head. Do not put the part in it until it is completely dry. Setting gel can be applied and the hair should be brushed back, away from the eyes, not straight down the sides of the head. This will help to train it so it won't fall over the eyes. The hair on the muzzle should always be brushed back toward the cheeks, *not* straight down.

The majority of experienced Silky Terrier fanciers advocate brushing a Silky's coat only after a bath since brushing a dry coat can cause hair breakage. For the best results when brushing between shampoos, spray the coat first with water, a creme rinse diluted with water, or a coat conditioner. You may want to blow dry the coat after brushing since a wet coat, when allowed to air dry, may become wavy.

Toenails should be trimmed regularly. They are too long if they touch the ground when the dog is standing. The nails are easiest to trim immediately after a bath when they have softened a little. Trim off a small amount at a time to avoid injuring the quick. There are products available to stop any bleeding should you injure it. Some Silky Terriers do not like having their toenails trimmed, so this should not be done on the table where they are groomed. Trim them elsewhere so they will not associate the table with something they dislike.

Silkys are one of the breeds that are tabled in the show ring. This means that the judge will examine each dog while it is standing still on a table, usually a grooming table. Pleasant grooming experiences on the table will make this part of the show training easy.

The hairs at the inside corners of the eyes can be shortened by hand plucking or by using thinning shears to remove any that touch or partially obscure the eyes. Using scissors in this area will not result in a natural look. Practice, and perhaps advice from experienced Silky exhibitors, will help you perfect techniques that enable your dog to look its best.

The Silky Terrier's teeth should be checked frequently for any buildup of tartar. Many veterinarians now advocate brushing dogs' teeth daily to maintain better dental health. They may also recommend products to reduce tartar formation.

Hand plucking the long hairs on the ears produces the best results. Pluck only a few hairs at a time. The remaining short hairs on the ears will have a velvety look and feel. The hair on the edges of the ears can be trimmed with scissors, if necessary. The inside of the ears should be kept clean with alcohol, or a commercially available product, used on cotton balls or swabs. Be extremely careful if it is necessary to use swabs to clean wax accumulation in the ears; it is possible to injure ear drums if the ears are probed too deeply.

Some Silkys have hair that is not easily hand plucked. This is often found on those with incorrect coat texture. If the hair does not break off easily by plucking, or if there is bare skin where it has been plucked, you are either doing it incorrectly or the dog should not be hand plucked. In this case thinning shears should be used instead.

The breed Standard calls for the Silky to have cat-like feet. Trimming the outline of the feet with scissors should result in a rounded foot with enough hair remaining so toenails and individual

Groomed and ready for the show ring is Ch. Larkspur
Tuckaway Angel, owned by Carolyn Stewart. Then . . .

. . . seconds later, after a vigorous shake of the head.
Thornton

Specialty Best of Breed winner Ch. Amron's Silver Sassafras (by Ch. Amron's Junior Mint Bear out of Ch. Luxa's Punkin' Patch of Amron). Bred by Norma Baugh and owned by Denor Hey and Beverly Bristol. *Nicole Macdurr*

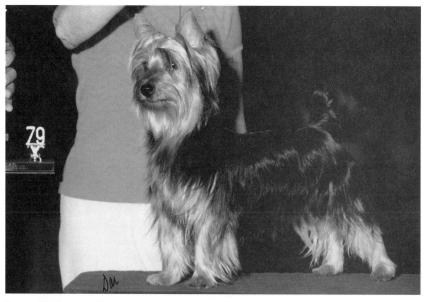

Future Ch. Redway Reggie Hampton (by Ch. Rebel Dandy Andy out of Ch. Redway Wexford Peter's Poppy), at ten months of age winning Best of Opposite Sex in Sweepstakes at the City of Angels Silky Terrier Club Specialty show in 1979. Bred and owned by Peggy Smith. *Rubin*

toes don't show. This look is achieved by leaving slightly more than a quarter of an inch of hair on the feet.

Clippers should *never* be used for show grooming. Pluck or use thinning shears to shorten any long hair up to the wrist on the front legs and up to the hock joint on the back of the rear legs. Long hair on the front of the rear legs may have to be shortened with thinning shears so it doesn't obscure the feet. The same is true of the long hair on the back of the front legs. By trimming in this manner, a natural look should be achieved that cannot be accomplished by using scissors.

Any shortening of the hair on the tail should result in an untrimmed appearance. This often takes practice but can be accomplished by using thinning shears, scissors or both. Enough hair should be left to balance nicely with the length of body coat. This will usually be from one to one and a half inches. *Do not remove too much.* A "stick tail" is not appropriate on a long-coated breed. If your Silky's tail was docked too short, you may want to leave a bit more hair on the end of the tail to make it appear longer.

Silky Terriers should not have coats that approach floor length. Too much emphasis is often placed on the coat length. Excessive length is neither required nor desirable. If your dog's coat is too long use thinning shears, never scissors, to remove the excess length. The coat should look natural, not abruptly chopped off, as is the case if scissors are used.

You may encounter the expression "put the dog in oil." This is unnecessary if your dog is receiving proper nutrition and coat care, and is free from parasites. Be warned, however: just one flea on a Silky can cause the dog to chew or scratch out hair.

GROOMING THE PET SILKY TERRIER

The majority of Silky Terriers in the dog show rings are also their owners' pets. Even if your Silky is not going to be shown you may prefer to groom it as outlined for the show dog. Bathing instructions are covered in that section. Not all Silkys like the bathing procedure, but they do enjoy being clean. You will be convinced of this when you observe their activity after they have been bathed and groomed.

Some owners of pet Silkys prefer to leave the long hair on the ears and feet. Detailed grooming is certainly unnecessary unless the hair impairs the dog in any way.

A regular schedule should be kept for grooming. The eyes, inside of the ears, toenails and teeth should be checked and attended to as described previously for the show dog.

If you find that maintaining the coat of your Silky becomes a chore for either of you, the dog can be trimmed in a "schnauzer" or other pet trim. This is the only time electric clippers should be used on a Silky. If you live in a cold weather area you should either time the trim so the dog's coat is longer during the cold weather or put a doggy sweater on him when he is outdoors.

12

Showing the Silky Terrier

AT AMERICAN KENNEL CLUB EVENTS there are two types of competition for dogs: Obedience and Conformation. This chapter concerns Conformation judging.

Conformation classes are those in which the judge examines the dog's conformation, condition, and temperament. The equipment needed to begin training is a show lead, a table to stand the dog on and a supply of treats to be used as rewards.

Various types of show leads are available. They serve as both collar and leash. You will need a lightweight one, about one-quarter inch wide, long enough to comfortably hold in your hand. The typical show lead will be made of nylon, leather or a tightly woven fabric, and it will have a locking slide that is adjustable at the neck. The lead should be an unobtrusive color that does not detract from your dog. Choke chain collars and those with buckles are not used in the Conformation ring. Buckled collars will wear off the hair around the neck. Choke chain collars may be used for obedience training but should never be left on an unattended dog.

Lead training should be started at an early age for Conforma-

Table training puppies for the show ring is essential. Shown is Loa Del Rey's Lea Lea (by Ch. Redway Danny Boy O'Wexford out of Ch. Centarra's Loa Oi), bred and owned by Adel Sievers and Pam Laperruque.

A Silky undergoes physical Conformation judging on an examination table. The judge is Katherine Gately examining future Ch. Weeblu's Windsong of Joy, CD (by Ch. Silti's Joy Boy out of Silkallure Wee One), handled by Peggy Lawson, who co-owned her with breeder Florence Males.

142

tion competition. The first two things a puppy should be taught are to walk beside you and to stand still comfortably on a table. To get a puppy accustomed to having something around its neck, you can make a collar out of ribbon or yarn. When the puppy is at ease with this collar, you can introduce the show lead. Fasten it around the puppy's neck, allowing about a finger's width between the slide and the neck. Gather up the remaining portion and secure it with a rubber band. The puppy will adjust to the additional weight and be able to go where it chooses. Do not leave the puppy alone while it has the lead around its neck.

The transition should be fairly easy from this step to the next. Unravel the lead and begin to guide the puppy's direction with it. Make it fun for the pup by offering words of encouragement and treats. If it shows any reluctance, you should reward it for taking just a few steps at first. Then remove the lead and play with the puppy. The next day try to get it to go a few more steps, and give more rewards. If the training sessions are brief and fun, the puppy will be walking properly on the lead within a short time.

In the show ring the dog will usually be walked on your left side. There are times, however, when you will probably be required to walk him on your right. The lead should be held in your corresponding hand. Be sure the dog is at ease walking on either side.

Silky Terriers should appear to be showing themselves. This can only be accomplished by training them to gait on a loose lead. This means that the lead should have a barely discernible amount of slack in it—just enough for you to have immediate control if the dog lowers its head when it is gaiting or standing. The lead should not be held taut. This is called stringing up, and it prevents the dog's free and easy movement.

With their terrier dispositions, Silkys should not be expected to stand like statues in the show ring. Silky Terriers look their best when shown as terriers are—with the handler standing rather than kneeling, which is the practice in the majority of toy breeds.

Pleasant early grooming experiences should make it simple to train the puppy for the table examination by the judge in the show ring. Put it on a table with a nonslip surface. When it remains still, even if just for a short time, praise it and give it a treat. When it is standing comfortably, put a show lead on it. Proceed with one step at a time and reward the puppy for each that is correctly performed.

Begin by placing the puppy's legs with the feet pointing forward, not turned in or out. The front legs should be well under the

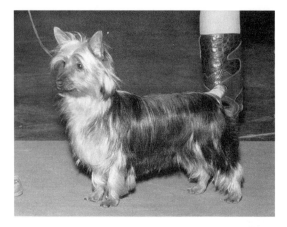

A Puppy class picture of soon-to-be Ch. Cantell Mercedes, showing herself as terriers should—without hand stacking. She was bred by Mary Lee Hendee and Stanley Matsumoto, and is owned by Mary Lee Hendee and Karen Schultz.
Booth

While lined up during competition this Silky is showing himself. Awaiting the judge's eye is Ch. Redway For Pete's Sake, bred and owned by Peggy Smith. *Arthur Fukumoto*

Group and Specialty Best of Opposite Sex winner Ch. Tri-K Kamelot of Sedgefield (by Ch. Centarra's Criterion out of Ch. Kiku's Tri-K Kriss-Miss Holly). Bred by Kriss and Kirstin Griffin and owned by Adel and Raymond Sievers. *Missy*

Am. and Can. Shoshana Alexander the Great (by Ch. Keneko's Gabby's Prince Blue out of Kiku's Shoshana's Misty Rose). Bred by Susan Mezistrano and owned by her and Leon Mezistrano.

Specialty winner Ch. Saturn's Jack Be Quick, CD (by Ch. Cypress Mi-Ohn Bosun out of Ch. Royaline Georgette of De Amo). Bred and owned by Jean Eliker. *Wayne Cott*

Group-winning Ch. Amron's Sensasha Bear II (by Ch. Amron's Hug-A-Bear out of Miss Robi Manhattan). Bred by Lisa Griffin and owned by Tom Baugh. *Luis F. Sosa*

146

body, and the rear legs should be placed so that the hocks are perpendicular to the table. Hold the head up with the lead and, if necessary, hold the tail upright. If the puppy is happy and relaxed, it will hold its tail up without your assistance. The object is to have the dog standing comfortably in this position with its topline straight, its ears up and with an interested expression. Practice by having someone gently run their hands over its body.

Once your puppy has had its inoculations against diseases, an excellent way of learning to handle it in the show ring is to attend conformation handling classes. These are offered by dog clubs and individuals. Such classes provide the opportunity to socialize your puppy and to have strangers examine it on the table. This acquaints the dog with having its teeth examined, and will accustom it to having its testicles checked.

AKC rules specify that only those dogs with two normal testicles, normally located in the scrotum, are eligible for competition in Conformation judging. These classes will also teach you the gaiting patterns that may be used in the show ring.

You will probably encounter various gaiting patterns. Some judges will ask you to move your dog "down and back." This is gaiting the dog in a straight line away from the judge and then back to him or her. Others may ask you to move your dog in a triangle or an "L"; these two are self-explanatory. When returning to the judge, on the completion of gaiting your dog, don't make the mistake of stopping the dog too close to the judge. Stop it two to three feet in front of the judge so that he or she can easily view it without having to step back.

Baiting your puppy can be a very effective means of having it pose. Various treats can be used to get, and keep, its attention. Give it the treat only when it is standing at attention, not if it lunges for it. Baiting takes practice and patience.

When your puppy has learned the basics, your next training grounds should be at a type of dog show known as a match. These are informal events that offer ring experience to dogs, their handlers and judges. Many matches have classes for puppies as young as two or three months of age. Seasoned exhibitors also take advantage of matches to train their puppies. Much can be learned by watching the experienced handlers in the ring.

When your Silky is six months old, it is eligible to be entered at American Kennel Club shows where championship points are awarded. Dogs that have been spayed or castrated can only be entered in Obedience competition.

Best in Show winner Ch. Fawn Hill the Donnybrook (by Ch. Nowifl's Best O'Luck out of Fawn Hill Roxanne). Bred by Verna Tucker and Eleanor Norton and owned by Verna Tucker.

Whether your Silky is entered at a match or a championship show, you should plan to arrive at least one hour before the scheduled time for breed judging. This will allow you time to groom your dog without rushing and an opportunity to exercise it before entering the ring.

Your handling skills and enjoyment of the sport will be increased if you stay at the show to watch other breeds in competition and study the handling of experienced exhibitors.

Showing dogs is rarely a profitable hobby, but it can be a rewarding experience when you and your Silky enjoy yourselves. At dog shows you will meet people with similar interests, and lifelong friendships are often made.

The winner of six Bests in Show, Ch. Cantell Heard A Rumor (by Ch. Silky Acres Magic Michael out of Martin's Lucky Comet). Bred by F. and C. Pierson and owned by Mary Lee Hendee and Delores Streng. *Booth*

13

The Winners' Circle

THE FOLLOWING is a chronicle of some of the most prestigious wins recorded by Silky Terriers since the breed was admitted to show competition in 1959. Included are the names of all Silkys that have won an all-breed Best in Show, the Best of Breed and Best of Opposite winners at the Silky Terrier Club of America Specialties and the Best of Breed winners at the Westminster Kennel Club shows.

ALL-BREED BEST IN SHOW WINNERS

1967 CH. MIDLAND'S JAN'S WENDY ANNE (bitch)
    (by Ch. Koonoona Bo Bo out of Ch. Lylac Jan)
1968 CH. KOONOONA BO BO* (dog)
    (by Bowenvale Midgey out of Aus. Ch. Brenhill Wee Julie)
    CH. HARGILL'S JOLLY JAMBOREE—2 BIS (dog)
    (by Ch. Wilhaven's Wee Sweet William out of Ch. Rebel
      Dancing Angel)
1970 CH. BONNEEN'S ARUNTA CHIEFTAIN (dog)
    (by Tamworth Cal out of Bonneen Blue Mist)

(*indicates imported)

Shown here at nine months of age is the first Silky Terrier Best in Show winner in the United States, Ch. Midland's Jan's Wendy Anne (by Ch. Koonoona Bo Bo out of Champion Lylac Jan). Bred and owned by Carmen Cananzi. *E. H. Frank*

The first multiple Best in Show winner, Ch. Hargill's Jolly Jamboree (by Ch. Wilhaven's Wee Sweet William out of Ch. Rebel Dancing Angel). Bred and owned by Harriett Gill. *Shafer*

1971 CH. GEM-G'S KOOL HAND LUKE (dog)
   (by Hayes Junior De La Ek out of Hayes Lady Tina De La
      Kreaux)
   CH. LYLAC BLUE PRINCE* (dog)
   (by Lylac Playboy out of Prairie Dail)
1972 CH. LYLAC BLUE PRINCE*—4 BIS (dog)
   (by Lylac Playboy out of Prairie Dail)
1973 CH. SHANIS KOALA SPORT (dog)
   (by Coolaroo Lord Montgomery III out of Ch. Shanis La
      Contessa Du Casey)
   CH. LYLAC BLUE PRINCE* (dog)
   (by Lylac Playboy out of Prairie Dail)
   CH. ROYALINE DON JUAN OF CASANOVA (dog)
   (by Ch. Silkallure Casanova out of Eilart Shadee Lady)
1974 CH. ROYALINE DON JUAN OF CASANOVA—6 BIS
      (dog)
   (by Ch. Silkallure Casanova out of Eilart Shadee Lady)
   CH. SHANIS KOALA SPORT—4 BIS (dog)
   (by Coolaroo Lord Montgomery III out of Ch. Shanis La
      Contessa Du Casey)
1975 CH. ASLETT'S KIKU'S BLUE STREAKER (dog)
   (by Ch. Hargill's Jolly Jamboree out of Ch. Kiku's St.
      Nick's Vixen)
1976 CH. WEEBLU'S BLAZE OF JOY (dog)
   (by Ch. Silti's Joy Boy out of Ch. Silkallure Wee One)
   CH. NOWIFL'S BEST O'LUCK (dog)
   (by Ch. Royaline Don Juan of Casanova out of Ch. Fawn
      Hill the Lucky Spot)
1977 CH. NOWIFL'S BEST O'LUCK (dog)
   (by Ch. Royaline Don Juan of Casanova out of Ch. Fawn
      Hill the Lucky Spot)
1979 CH. CASA DE CASEY TOUCH OF CLASS (dog)
   (by Ch. Silkallure Casanova out of Eilart Shadee Lady)
   CH. FAWN HILL THE DONNYBROOK (dog)
   (by Ch. Nowifl's Best O'Luck out of Fawn Hill Roxanne)
1980 CH. WEEBLU'S BLAZE OF JOY (dog)
   (by Ch. Silti's Joy Boy out of Ch. Silkallure Wee One)
   CH. WEEBLU'S TRAILBLAZER OF DON-EL—3 BIS
      (dog)
   (by Ch. Weeblu's Blaze of Joy out of Ch. Don-El's Too
      Good To Be True)

Ch. Bowenvale Coralee (by Bowenvale Blue Bill out of Dainty Girl), a Best of Breed winner, from the classes, at the Silky Terrier Club of America Specialty in 1968. Bred in Australia by Eric Fellows and owned by Frances Van Etten.

Best in Show and Specialty Best of Breed winner Aus., Can. and Am. Ch. Koonoona Bo Bo (by Bowenvale Midgey out of Aus. Ch. Brenhill Wee Julie). Bred by Mrs. P. Brown and owned by Carmen Cananzi.

1981 CH. WEEBLU'S TRAILBLAZER OF DON-EL—2 BIS (dog)
(by Ch. Weeblu's Blaze of Joy out of Ch. Don-El's Too Good To Be True)
CH. CANTELL HEARD A RUMOR—2 BIS (dog)
(by Ch. Silky Acres Magic Michael out of Martin's Lucky Comet)
CH. ROSEWELL'S BLUE DIAMOND GEM (dog)
(by Ch. Rosewell's My Blue Shadow out of Midnight Lady)
1982 CH. CANTELL HEARD A RUMOR—4 BIS (dog)
(by Ch. Silky Acres Magic Michael out of Martin's Lucky Comet)
CH. WEEBLU'S TRAILBLAZER OF DON-EL—2 BIS (dog)
(by Ch. Weeblu's Blaze of Joy out of Ch. Don-El's Too Good To Be True)
CH. WYNCREST ELI'S SON—2 BIS (dog)
(by Ch. Lu-Jon's Wyncrest Soul Brother out of Ch. Lu-Jon's Wyncrest Bad Banshee)
1983 CH. FAWN HILL LUCKNOW SWEET N'SOUR (bitch)
(by Ch. Rita's Firebrand of Fawn Hill out of Ch. Fawn Hill Sweet Rosie O'Grady)
1985 CH. WEEBLU'S TRAILBLAZER OF DON-EL (dog)
(by Ch. Weeblu's Blaze of Joy out of Ch. Don-El's Too Good To Be True)
CH. FAWN HILL LUCKNOW SWEET N'SOUR (bitch)
(by Ch. Rita's Firebrand of Fawn Hill out of Ch. Fawn Hill Sweet Rosie O'Grady)

SILKY TERRIER CLUB OF AMERICA NATIONAL SPECIALTY WINNERS

(Listed first is Best of Breed, second is Best of Opposite Sex)

1961 CH. WARATAH WALKABOUT (dog)
(by Waratah Ramble out of Chota Grenadine)
CH. BOWENVALE MARGIE* (bitch)
(by Aus. Ch. Bowenvale Sir Rex out of Mammon Princess Dawn)

1962 BILLABONG TINY TIM (dog)
   (by Ch. Coolaroo Sir Winston out of Coolaroo Lady
   Penny)
   CH. BOWENVALE MARGIE* (bitch)
   (by Aus. Ch. Bowenvale Sir Rex out of Mammon Princess
   Dawn)
1963 CH. BOWENVALE BLUE BOY* (dog)
   (by Aus. Ch. Bo Bo out of Dainty Girl)
   CH. BOWENVALE MARGIE* (bitch)
   (by Aus. Ch. Bowenvale Sir Rex out of Mammon Princess
   Dawn)
1964 CH. SILKALLURE GINO MIO (dog)
   (by Ch. Coolaroo Sir Winston out of Ch. Silkallure
   Rexanne)
   CH. MAV-ROB LADY CAMELOT (bitch)
   (by Ch. Fair Dinkum Maverick, CD, out of Victoria
   Wendy Regina)
1965 SILKALLURE CASANOVA (dog)
   (by Ch. Coolaroo Sir Winston out of Bondoon's Silkie
   Sullivan)
   CH. ALDOON BONNIE LASS* (bitch)
   (by Aus. Ch. Aldoon Sivam out of Aldoon Lassie)
1966 CH. TINKER BLUE BLAZES (dog)
   (by Ch. Fair Dinkum Maverick, CD, out of Silturn Blue
   Dawn)
   CH. LYLAC JAN* (bitch)
   (by Leroy Misty out of Aldoon Wendy Ann)
1967 CH. REDWAY BONNIE LASS (bitch)
   (by Ch. Wexford Pogo out of Redway Rebecca)
   CH. MARA'S SILVER BEGGAR BOY (dog)
   (by Ch. Redway Beau Brummell out of Ch. Maras Tiny
   Tuppence)
1968 (West) BOWENVALE CORALEE* (bitch)
   (by Bowenvale Blue Bill out of Dainty Girl)
   CH. CASA DE CASEY MATE O'THE MIST (dog)
   (by Ch. Silkallure Casanova out of Silkallure Molly Brown)
1968 (East) CH. FAWN HILL THE SOROBAN (dog)
   (by Ch. Larrakin Gorgeous George out of Larrakin Young
   Betty)
   CH. BOWENVALE CORALEE (bitch)
   (by Bowenvale Blue Bill out of Dainty Girl)

1969 (East) CH. FAWN HILL THE SOROBAN (dog)
   (by Ch. Larrakin Gorgeous George out of Larrakin Young
      Betty)
   CH. KOONOONA CO LODI* (bitch)
   (by Koonoona Mr. Pip out of Koonoona Gina Mia)
1969 (West) CH. SILKALLURE TADJI (dog)
   (by Ch. Silkallure Casanova out of Ch. Silkallure
      Rexalinda)
   CH. KRISKAH MISTE OF REXANDY (bitch)
   (by Ch. Silkallure Rexandy out of Night Mist of the
      Valley)
1970 (East) CH. KOONOONA BO BO* (dog)
   (by Bowenvale Midgey out of Aus. Ch. Brenhill Wee Julie)
   CH. SOBLU MY FANCY (bitch)
   (by Ch. Midland's Fancy Frankie out of Ch. Just a
      Smidgen of Dixie)
1970 (West) CH. LU-JON'S LORD CAGNEY OF TUNNEY
      (dog)
   (by Ch. Bonneen's Arunta Chieftain out of Brandy of
      Tunney)
   CH. SOBLU MY FANCY (bitch)
   (by Ch. Midland's Fancy Frankie out of Ch. Just a
      Smidgen of Dixie)
1971 (West) CH. GEM-G'S KOOL HAND LUKE (dog)
   (by Hayes Junior De La Ek out of Hayes Lady Tina De La
      Kreaux)
   CH. SOBLU MY FANCY (bitch)
   (by Ch. Midland's Fancy Frankie out of Ch. Just a
      Smidgen of Dixie)
1971 (East) CH. LU-JON'S LORD CAGNEY OF TUNNEY
      (dog)
   (by Ch. Bonneen's Arunta Chieftain out of Brandy of
      Tunney)
   CH. SOBLU MY FANCY (bitch)
   (by Ch. Midland's Fancy Frankie out of Ch. Just a
      Smidgen of Dixie)
1972 (East) CH. MILL CREEK'S LIL BEAU BLUE (dog)
   (by Ch. Koonoona Bo Bo out of Ch. Bumblebee of Iradell)
   CH. BONNIE LASS OF SYDNEY (bitch)
   (by Prince Choco out of Silver Blue Belle)
1972 (West) CH. SULE SKERRY TADJIS DE MARIA (dog)
   (by Ch. Silkallure Tadji out of Silkallure Poussi G'Lour)

Ch. Royaline Don Juan of Casanova (by Ch. Silkallure Casanova out of Eilart Shadee Lady) won six Bests in Show. He was also a Specialty Best of Breed and Iradell Trophy winner. Bred by Victor and Mona Bracco and owned by Robert and Gloria Farron. *Henry*

Best in Show and STCA Specialty Best of Breed winner Ch. Weeblu's Blaze of Joy (by Ch. Silti's Joy Boy out of Ch. Silkallure Wee One). Bred and owned by Florence Males. *Bergman*

Best in Show winner Ch. Aslett's Kiki's Blue Streaker (by Ch. Hargill's Jolly Jamboree out of Ch. Kiku's St. Nick's Vixen). Bred by Kay Magnussen and Janet Aslett, owned by Jon and Kay Magnussen, and handled by Jerry Moon. *Roberts*

MOONFLEET CLEMENTINA (bitch)
(by Ch. Silkallure Rexandy out of Thackaringa Clemmie)
1973 (West) CH. LYLAC BLUE PRINCE* (dog)
(by Lylac Playboy out of Prairie Dail)
CH. DON-EL'S LOOK OF ELEGANCE (bitch)
(by Ch. Silkallure Casanova out of Princess Parizade)
1973 (East) CH. MIDLAND'S BLUE MISSY (bitch)
(by Ch. Mill Creek's Lil' Beau Blue out of Bluiltan
Duchess Silver Lady)
CH. THE SILKEN PEPPY DIGGER (dog)
(by Montrose Berkley out of Hazelmar Candy)
1974 CH. LYLAC BLUE PRINCE* (dog)
(by Lylac Playboy out of Prairie Dail)
CH. ROSEWELL'S POLLAE OF BABY DOE (bitch)
(by Ch. Tinker Blue Blazes out of Azulada of Baby Doe)
1975 CH. SHANIS KOALA SPORT (dog)
(by Coolaroo Lord Montgomery III out of Ch. Shanis La
Contessa Du Casey)
CH. DON-EL'S LOOK OF ELEGANCE (bitch)
(by Ch. Silkallure Casanova out of Princess Parizade)
1976 CH. ROYALINE DON JUAN OF CASANOVA (dog)
(by Ch. Silkallure Casanova out of Eilart Shadee Lady)
CH. STARHO'S CASA DE CASEY KOALA (bitch)
(by Ch. Casa De Casey Special Edition out of Lady Bird
Beetle Of Coolaroo)
1977 CH. KIKU'S JJ JAMBOREE, CD (dog)
(by Ch. Hargill's Jolly Jamboree out of Ch. Wym Wey
with a Wag)
CH. JODAS KOALAS MISS MUFFY (bitch)
(by Ch. Koala I'm Casey's Dandy out of Ch. Royaline
Princess Muffy)
1978 CH. GRIZEBECK CHANTILLY (bitch)
(by Ch. Lu-Jon's Gabby Baby out of Lu-Jon's Moonlight of
Kaduna)
CH. MIDLAND'S KOONOONA BLUE MIKE (dog)
(by Ch. Midland's Mighty Mike out of Midland
Koonoona's Dolly-Di)
1979 CH. ROSEWELL'S POLLAE OF BABY DOE (bitch)
(by Ch. Tinker Blue Blazes out of Azulada of Baby Doe)
CH. REDWAY WILLIE WAGTAIL (dog)
(by Ch. Silky Acres Dandy Dude out of Ch. Redway
Wexford Peter's Poppy)

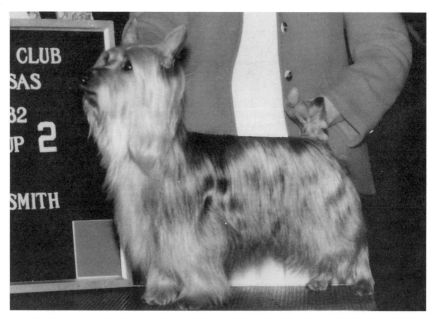

Best in Show winner Ch. Rosewell's Blue Diamond Gem (by Ch. Rosewell's My Blue Shadow out of Midnight Lady). Bred by M. R. Medina and owned by Louise Rosewell.   *Petrulis*

Best in Show and STCA Specialty Best of Breed winner Ch. Gem-G's Kool Hand Luke (by Hayes Junior De La Ek out of Hayes Lady Tina De La Kreaux). Bred by Joe Hayes and owned by James Green.   *Gilbert*

162

1980 CH. WEEBLU'S TRAILBLAZER OF DON-EL (dog)
(by Ch. Weeblu's Blaze of Joy out of Ch. Don-El's Too
Good To Be True)
CH. KENEKO'S SWEET LUCY O'WEEBLU (bitch)
(by Ch. Weeblu's Blaze of Joy out of Lloyd's Samantha)
1981 CH. WEEBLU'S TRAILBLAZER OF DON-EL (dog)
(by Ch. Weeblu's Blaze of Joy out of Ch. Don-El's Too
Good To Be True)
CH. WOODLYNND'S HECATE (bitch)
(by Ch. Kiku's Winalot Willie out of Woodlynnds Wee
Julee)
1982 CH. KOALA'S KATCH ME IF YOU KAN (dog)
(by Ch. Koala Toy Boy, CD out of Ch. Koala's Lovable
Tinkerbelle)
CH. FAWN HILL LUCKNOW SWEET N'SOUR (bitch)
(by Ch. Rita's Firebrand of Fawn Hill out of Ch. Fawn
Hill Sweet Rosie O'Grady)
1983 CH. WYNCREST ELI'S SON (dog)
(by Ch. Lu-Jon's Wyncrest Soul Brother out of Ch.
Lu-Jon's Wyncrest Bad Banshee)
CH. FAWN HILL WILD GINGER (bitch)
(by Ch. Rita's Firebrand of Fawn Hill out of Ch. Fawn
Hill Sweet Rosie O'Grady)
1984 CH. FAWN HILL LUCKNOW SWEET N'SOUR (bitch)
(by Ch. Rita's Firebrand of Fawn Hill out of Ch. Fawn
Hill Sweet Rosie O'Grady)
CH. REDWAY DANNY BOY O'WEXFORD (dog)
(by Ch. Silky Acres Dandy Dude out of Ch. Redway
Wexford Peter's Poppy)
1985 CH. FAWN HILL LUCKNOW SWEET N'SOUR (bitch)
(by Ch. Rita's Firebrand of Fawn Hill out of Ch. Fawn
Hill Sweet Rosie O'Grady)
CH. WEEBLU'S TRAILBLAZER OF DON-EL (dog)
(by Ch. Weeblu's Blaze of Joy out of Ch. Don-El's Too
Good To Be True)
1986 CH. FAWN HILL LUCKNOW SWEET N'SOUR (bitch)
(by Ch. Rita's Firebrand of Fawn Hill out of Ch. Fawn
Hill Sweet Rosie O'Grady)
CH. WEEBLU'S TRAILBLAZER OF DON-EL (dog)
(by Ch. Weeblu's Blaze of Joy out of Ch. Don-El's Too
Good To Be True)

1987 CH. SUNDANCE'S RAGTIME (dog)
  (by Ch. Cantell Heard a Rumor out of Cantell Tongue in
    Cheek, CD)
  CH. TESSIER DANIELLE OF SHOSHANA (bitch)
  (by Ch. Silwynd Apricot Cordial out of Ch. Kiku's
    Vivacious Vonda)
1988 CH. TRU BLU ZIGGY STARDUST (dog)
  (by Ch. Tru Blu Rumors A'Cookin out of Ch. Larkspurs
    Rustle of Taffeta)
  CH. CORMAT'S FASCINATION (bitch)
  (by Ch. Rita's Firebrand of Fawn Hill out of Cormat's
    Miss Kitty)
1989 CH. AMRON'S SILVER SASSAFRAS (bitch)
  (by Ch. Amron's Junior Mint Bear out of Ch. Luxa's
    Punkin' Patch of Amron)
  CH. SATURN'S JACK BE QUICK, CD (dog)
  (by Ch. Cypress Mi-Ohn Bosun out of Ch. Royaline
    Georgette of De Amo)

WESTMINSTER KENNEL CLUB
BEST OF BREED WINNERS

1960 CH. ALDOON COUNTESS CANDY* (bitch)
  (by Glenboig Tim out of Aldoon Lassie)
1961 CH. MILAN CHIPS OF IRADELL* (dog)
  (by Aus. Ch. Emeraldale Timothy out of Milan Lindy Lou)
1962 CH. REDWAY LORD MICHAEL (dog)
  (by Ch. Wexford Pogo out of Brenhill Splinters)
1963 MILAN MISS SANDRA OF IRADELL* (bitch)
  (by Aus. Ch. Milan Tony out of Milan Lindy Lou)
1964 CH. MILAN MISS SANDRA OF IRADELL*—Group 4
    (bitch)
  (by Aus. Ch. Milan Tony out of Milan Lindy Lou)
1965 CH. SILKALLURE KISS ME KATE (bitch)
  (by Ch. Coolaroo Sir Winston out of Ch. Bowenvale
    Margie)
1966 CH. SILKALLURE CASANOVA—Group 4 (dog)
  (by Ch. Coolaroo Sir Winston out of Bondoon's Silkie
    Sullivan)

(*indicates imported)

1967 CH. PRINCESS SUE OF IRADELL (bitch)
(by Ch. Lucky Prince of Iradell out of Ch. Milan Susanna)

1968 CH. SILKALLURE CASANOVA (dog)
(by Ch. Coolaroo Sir Winston out of Bondoon's Silkie Sullivan)

1969 CH. HARGILL'S JOLLY JAMBOREE (dog)
(by Ch. Wilhaven's Wee Sweet Wm. out of Ch. Rebel Dancing Angel)

1970 CH. GEM-G'S KOOL HAND LUKE (dog)
(by Hayes Junior De La Ek out of Hayes Lady Tina De La Kreaux)

1971 CH. BLUE ROGUE OF THE BRYN (dog)
(by Ch. Tinker Blue Blazes out of Ch. Silk Oaks Amy)

1972 CH. SILKALLURE TADJI (dog)
(by Ch. Silkallure Casanova out of Ch. Silkallure Rexalinda)

1973 CH. ROYALINE DON JUAN OF CASANOVA (dog)
(by Ch. Silkallure Casanova out of Eilart Shadee Lady)

1974 CH. ROYALINE DON JUAN OF CASANOVA (dog)
(by Ch. Silkallure Casanova out of Eilart Shadee Lady)

1975 CH. REDWAY FOR PETE'S SAKE (dog)
(by Ch. Gem-G's Kool Hand Luke out of Ch. Soblu My Fancy)

1976 CH. ROYALINE DON JUAN OF CASANOVA (dog)
(by Ch. Silkallure Casanova out of Eilart Shadee Lady)

1977 CH. NOWIFLS BEST O'LUCK (dog)
(by Ch. Royaline Don Juan of Casanova out of Ch. Fawn Hill the Lucky Spot)

1978 CH. REDWAY DANNY BOY O'WEXFORD (dog)
(by Ch. Silky Acres Dandy Dude out of Ch. Redway Wexford Peter's Poppy)

1979 CH. CYPRESS SKIPPER MI OHN (dog)
(by Ch. Cypress Townshend Lucky Lad out of Cypress Bee Jay)

1980 CH. WYNCREST TRUPENCE WOODSPRITE (bitch)
(by Ch. Koobala's Chivas Regal out of Ch. Lu-John's Wyncrest Bad Banshee)

1981 CH. WEEBLU'S TRAILBLAZER OF DON-EL (dog)
(by Ch. Weeblu's Blaze of Joy out of Ch. Don-El's Too Good To Be True)

The record holder with eight Bests in Show, Ch. Weeblu's Trailblazer of Don-El, pictured at ten months of age (by Ch. Weeblu's Blaze of Joy out of Ch. Don-El's Too Good To Be True). He is also a Specialty Best of Breed and Iradell Trophy winner. Bred by Don and Helen Thompson and owned by Florence Males. *Bill Francis*

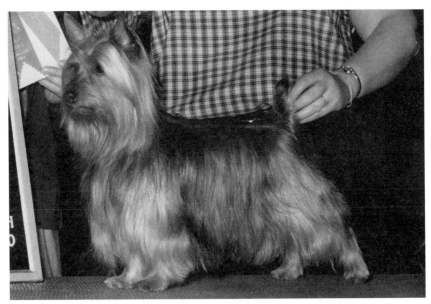

Best in Show and Specialty Best of Breed winner Ch. Wyncrest Eli's Son (by Ch. Lu-Jon's Wyncrest Soul Brother out of Ch. Lu-Jon's Wyncrest Bad Banshee). Bred and owned by Barbara Heckerman, co-owned by Jesse Pfeiffer, Jr. *Booth*

1982 CH. FAWN HILL SPENCER OF RIMMON (dog)
   (by Ch. Rita's Firebrand of Fawn Hill out of Ch. Fawn
   Hill Sweet Rosie O'Grady)

1983 CH. FAWN HILL LUCKNOW SWEET N'SOUR (bitch)
   (by Ch. Rita's Firebrand of Fawn Hill out of Ch. Fawn
   Hill Sweet Rosie O'Grady)

1984 CH. WYNCREST ELI'S SON (dog)
   (by Ch. Lu-Jon's Wyncrest Soul Brother out of Ch.
   Lu-Jon's Wyncrest Bad Banshee)

1985 CH. FAWN HILL LUCKNOW SWEET N'SOUR (bitch)
   (by Ch. Rita's Firebrand of Fawn Hill out of Ch. Fawn
   Hill Sweet Rosie O'Grady)

1986 CH. DAWNWIND'S AM I BLUE—Group 4 (dog)
   (by Koonoona Independence Bo Bo out of Dawnwind's
   Liza of Ronco)

1987 CH. FAWN HILL LUCKNOW SWEET N'SOUR (bitch)
   (by Ch. Rita's Firebrand of Fawn Hill out of Ch. Fawn
   Hill Sweet Rosie O'Grady)

1988 CH. DUNAR'S THOR OF SAFIRE (dog)
   (by Ch. Dunars Blu Blaz'r OTailswest out of Ch. Safire
   Trilby)

1989 CH. GLEN ROW LAPSITTER'S CRYSTAL (bitch)
   (by Ch. Lakewind Skip Jack out of Ch. Lapsitter's
   Pennyblue Spark)

1990 CH. ANOVA'S WYNCREST TRAVELER (dog)
   (by Ch. Koala's Katch Me If You Kan out of Ch. Anova's
   M'Lady Abigale)

Ch. Weeblu's Blazing Apollo, CDX (by Ch. Weeblu's Blaze of Joy out of Petite Joli Femme). Bred and owned by Helen and Evie Clark. *Jim Lawson*

14

The Silky Terrier in Obedience and Tracking

OBEDIENCE TRAINING is based on behavior modification: rewarding the dog for desirable behavior and correcting the dog when necessary. Praising your dog for correct performance is far more important.

OBEDIENCE

Many kennel clubs offer obedience training classes for dogs six months of age and older. Some even offer a very basic course for puppies three to six months old, commonly called kindergarten classes.

If you plan to enter your Silky in Obedience competition at dog shows, you should attend these classes. The instructor can see and point out errors that the handler is making but is not aware of.

The first Silky Terrier to gain an American Kennel Club title, Stroud Mandy Fowler, CD (by Aus. Ch. Stroud Willie John out of Stroud Estelle Brassey). She gained her title while the breed was still in the Miscellaneous class. She was bred by Mrs. Birkin-O'Donnell in Australia and imported and owned by Zell Fowler Neilson.

One of the first dual title holders, Ch. Redway Flying Timothy, CD (by Prairie Roger out of Ch. Redway Splinters). Bred by Peggy Smith and owned by Eleanor and Robert Franceschi. Eleanor Franceschi also gained the dual title on her Ch. Redway Black Eyed Susan.

Repeated handler errors are the main reason some dogs do not respond properly.

A Silky is a Toy breed, but it is also a terrier. All terrier breeds are considered to be real challenges in regard to formal obedience training. They are individuals, and each responds differently. Some do well with a nylon training collar; others require a chain collar. You will need to learn many different techniques. The number of Silkys with Obedience titles is proof that most enjoy obedience when trained with love, praise, patience, and understanding.

As of 1989, more than 300 American Silky Terriers have earned Obedience degrees. Many have earned the Companion Dog (CD) and Companion Dog Excellent (CDX) titles. Eighteen have gained the Utility Dog (UD) title and six have garnered the Tracking Dog (TD) degree. None have yet gained the Tracking Dog Excellent (TDX) degree.

The Companion Dog degree is earned at the Novice level of Obedience. The dog is required to heel on and off lead, stand for examination, and perform the recall (coming when called). The dog must also perform the long sit and long down, which requires it to stay in these positions for a specified period of time, on command, with the handler facing the dog on the other side of the ring.

The Companion Dog Excellent degree is attained in the next level of obedience competition. The dog heels without a lead and must drop on recall. This means it must, on command, lie down when coming to you. On further command the dog must come the rest of the way to you. It must retrieve a dumbbell from the floor and also after going over the high jump, and must return over the high jump. The dog must also jump a broad jump. In this competition the long sits and downs are for a longer period of time and the handlers are out of sight.

The Utility Dog title is the Ph.D. of Obedience degrees. The signal exercise requires the dog to respond only to hand signals for the heel, stand, down, sit and come. Scent discrimination requires the dog to use its nose to pick out one article, from among eight, which has been scented by the handler. This is done twice, once for metal and once for leather articles. In the directed retrieve the dog must go out and pick up one designated glove from three. The moving stand and examination exercise requires the dog to stop in a standing position while the handler goes to a designated spot and then go directly to heel position. In the directed jumping the dog must go against its natural instinct by leaving the handler and proceed in a straight line to the opposite end of the ring, sit on command and wait for further commands. It is then instructed to take a specific jump, either the high jump or the bar jump. This is then repeated for the other jump.

The first AKC Obedience-titled Silky Terrier was Stroud Mandy Fowler, CD, an Australian import owned by Zell Fowler Neilson. She gained the title in April 1958 when the breed was still in the Miscellaneous class.

In 1979 the Silky Terrier Club of America inaugurated a yearly award called the Stroud Mandy Fowler CD Trophy. As well as honoring her, it honors the top winning obedience Silky each year, based on a point scale according to the dog's Obedience scores at AKC shows.

The first winner of the trophy was the most titled Silky Terrier in the United States and, perhaps, in the world. He was Int., Am., Can., Mex., P.R. and Dom. Ch. Sonnyvale's Klown of Kamelot, Am. UDT, Can. CDX, Mex. CD, VB. The VB denotes passing a temperament test based on German rules. He did this at the first such testing in the United States. His sire was Ch. Casa De Casey Agil of Fawn Hill and his dam Ch. Sonnyvale's Trixanna Susanna, CD. He was owned by Frances and Boyd Johnson.

Klown's accomplishments were many in addition to his titles. He was the first Silky champion to earn the UD title and the first champion and second Silky to gain the TD degree. In 1976, when he was being shown in Canada, he was rated the number one Silky and the number ten toy dog in obedience in *Dogs in Canada* magazine. He was the subject of a nationally aired television program entitled "Kids' World" and appeared in a stage production of *The Wizard of Oz* as Toto. He was nearly eighteen years old when he died in 1988.

The recipients of the Stroud Mandy Fowler CD award since then have been:

1980, 1981, 1982, and 1983—Silti Braci Lin Houdini, UD, Mex. CDX, Temperament Tested (by Ch. Silti Tumbleweed Pete out of Silti's Tiger Rose of Trallee). She is owned by Linda Ann and Linda Louise Schulte.

1984—Ch. Silti's La Pixi Michilli, CDX (by Ch. Silti's Mr. Montague out of Ch. Silti's Saranade). Her owners, Gordon and Eleanor Schulte, are the parents of the Schulte sisters, who own the previous four-year winner! The family has been active with Silkys in Obedience since the mid-1960s. Their Lady Brandewyne completed her UD degree in 1969, and

Kindergarten obedience training! Nine-week-old Amron's Harper's Bearzaar, owned by Barbara Fraus and her breeder, Norma Baugh.

Aus. Ch. Karribi Blue Sensation, CDX, in action. Bred and owned by Joan Geogeghan of Victoria, Australia. *Photography by Neilson*

Taking the **broad jump** is Silti Braci Lin Houdini, Am. UD, Mex. CDX. Bred by Mary Estrin and owned by Linda Ann and Linda Louise Schulte.

On the right is Ch. Tru Blu Bei Under My Spell, UD, with her sixteen-month-old daughter Khara's Abby of Windemere. Abby is co-owned by her breeder, Linda Hart, with Sandra and W. G. Opie.

was the second Silky to gain this title in the United States. Their Soblu Brockaway Houdini, CDX, was one of only six with this title when he gained it in 1968.

1985, 1986, and 1988—Ch. Tru Blu Bei Under My Spell, UD (by Ch. Blu-N-Tan Shadow Magic out of Ch. Larkspurs Rustle of Taffeta). Owner handled by Linda K. Hart.

1987—Kamelot's Klever Kaper Dakota, Am. and Can. CDX (by Klown, the 1979 winner, out of Ch. Sunnyvale's Song Sung Blue, CD. He is owned by Ann E. Will.

The eighteen Silkys that have gained the UD title and their year of completion are:

Mabrouka Eamonn, UD (by Peterborough Spin out of Rolinda Miss Bamby), owned by Ernest and Alicia Hanschman, 1961

Lady Brandewyne, UD (by Connemara Grogan Kinsella out of Selecta Saucy Sal), owned by Gordon and Eleanor Schulte, 1969

Harwal's Abou-Ben-Adham, UD (by Ch. Tinker Blue Blazes out of Totham Miss Ginny Jo), owned by Harry Wallach, 1970

Queen Cindy Out of Eileen, UD (by Peanuts out of Sister of Eileen), owned by Dorothy Huber, 1970

Oonbou Dinky of Sydney, UDT (by Ch. Koonoona Lord Sydney out of Ch. Koonoona Co Lodi), owned by Connie Alber, 1973

Ch. Sonnyvale's Klown of Camelot, UDT (by Ch. Casa De Casey Agil of Fawn Hill out of Ch. Sonnyvale's Trixanna Susanna, CD.), owned by Frances and Boyd Johnson, 1975

Ch. Ronnsown Sparkling Scamp, UD (by Ch. Midland's Beau O'Ronhoff out of Ch. Ronnsown Beaudette O'Ronhoff), owned by Patricia Ward and Helen O'Neill, 1976

Oonbou's Foolish Pleasure, UDT (by Ch. Lynhaven's Timmy Taco O'El Toro out of Ch. Oonbou's Aruma Royal Muffin), owned by Connie Alber, 1978

Lady Allegra Bannon, UD (by Sir Jasper Bannon out of Lady Misty Bannon), owned by Louise Fox, 1981

Trelew's Lady Tina Marie, UD (by Ch. Fawn Hill Gadabout out of Sonnyvale's Lady Deanne), owned by J. Dice, 1981

Halaine Jon Boy of Pauoa, UD (by Junal Mai Ti Koi Silkallure out of Valanne Lady Susan), owned by N. and J. Sanada, 1982

Silti Braci Lin Houdini, UD (by Ch. Silti Tumbleweed Pete out

Int., Am., Can., Mex., P.R. and Dom. Ch. Sonnyvale's Klown of Kamelot, Am. UDT, Can. CDX, Mex. CD, the most titled Silky Terrier in the United States. Bred by Janet and John Matthews and owned by Frances and Boyd Johnson.

Ch. Saturn's Io, CD, pictured in an Obedience **long down**. Bred and owned by Jean Eliker. She is an example of Silky Terrier versatility: a family member, a show dog, an Obedience Trial competitor and the dam of champions.

Ch. Tru Blue Bei Under My Spell, UD, performs at an obedience fun demonstration with her owner Linda Hart at the Denver Foreign Film Festival. She has also won two all-breed High in Trial awards.

Ch. Ronnsown Sparkling Scamp, UD, was the first of her sex to acquire the two titles. She was bred by Ron Hartright-Leighton and owned by Patricia Ward and Helen O'Neill.

Oonbou Dinky of Sydney, UDT, the first Silky Terrier to earn a Tracking Dog title. He was bred and owned by Connie Alber.

of Silti's Tiger Rose of Trallee), owned by Linda Ann and Linda Louise Schulte, 1984

Sharinga Sukitu, UD (by Ch. Austral Blu Beau Jangles out of Ch. Austral Lyn-Dee of D'Bab), owned by L. Alan and A. Lundgren, 1985

Tru Blu Pride N Joy, UD (by Ch. Silti's Joy Boy out of Ch. Larkspurs Rustle of Taffeta), owned by G. Clark, 1985

Ch. Tru Blu Bei Under My Spell, UD (by Ch. Blu-N-Tan Shadow Magic out of Ch. Larkspurs Rustle of Taffeta), owned by Linda Hart and Linda Mowrer, 1985

Ch. Tails West Tammy, UD (by Ch. Tails-West Hi-Tony out of Ch. Bludure's Cinderella Du Casey), owned by Dorothy Huber, 1987

Chrisbonli's Sky Cat, UD (by Chrisbonli's Hold That Tiger out of Chrisbonli's Out for Glory), owned by Joan C. Woodward and Girdley and Paula Huff, 1988

Birubi's Arika Caroo, UD (by Woodlynnd's Mighty Timothy out of Tilly), owned by Jocelyn Fraser, 1988

Dorothy Huber's Ch. Tails West Tammy, UD, is a good example of the breed's soundness of mind and body well past middle age. She completed her UD title three months after her eleventh birthday. A perfect score in Obedience is 200 points. Tammy came close with her three qualifying scores of 195, 190 and 194. Owners whose Silkys score in the high 190s can be very proud of their dogs—and themselves. Tammy has taken High in Trial at the 1980 Silky Terrier Club of America Specialty and at three City of Angels Silky Terrier Club Specialties.

TRACKING

Obtaining the title of Tracking Dog (TD) is undeniably a very challenging endeavor for a Silky owner. The purpose of Tracking Tests, as described in the American Kennel Club's *Obedience Regulations,* is:

> to demonstrate the dog's ability to recognize and follow human scent and to use this skill in the service of mankind.
>
> Tracking, by its nature, is a vigorous noncompetitive outdoor sport. Tracking Tests should demonstrate willingness and enjoyment by the dog in his work and should always represent the best in sportsmanship and camaraderie by the people involved.
>
> The Regulations require that each track be designed to test dog and handler with a variety of terrain and scenting conditions. The dog is

not asked to find the tracklayer, but he must overcome a series of typical scenting problems and locate objects dropped by the person whose track is being followed.

A track in Tracking Dog competition is required to extend at least 440 yards to 500 yards (a little more than a quarter of a mile), with a leather glove or wallet dropped at the end of the track. The track must have at least two right-angle turns and be at least one-half hour old. In Tracking Dog Excellent competition the track must be no less than 800 yards and no longer than 1,000 yards. It will have more turns, cover all types of terrain and ground cover and be at least three hours old.

Six American Silkys have earned the TD degree, one being the previously mentioned multi-titled Ch. Sonnyvale's Klown of Kamelot, UDT. The other five were all owned by Connie Alber. She finished her first Obedience-titled Silky in 1968 and is now approved by the AKC to judge all Obedience classes, as well as the TD and TDX tests. Her years of experience have convinced her that Silkys are good little trackers and enjoy the Tracking Dog competition. She would like to see more owners become involved in this sport.

The six Silkys that have gained the TD title and their year of completion are:

Oonbou Dinky of Sydney, UDT (by Ch. Koonoona Lord Sydney out of Ch. Koonoona Co Lodi), 1975

Oonbou Osh Gosh, CDT (by Ch. Koonoona Lord Sydney out of Ch. Koonoona Co Lodi), 1977

Ch. Sonnyvale's Klown of Kamelot, UDT (by Ch. Casa De Casey Agil of Fawn Hill out of Ch. Sonnyvale's Trixanna Susanna, CD), 1978

Ch. Oonbou's Mitte Decem-Tales, TD (by Ch. Koonoona Lord Sydney out of Ch. Koonoona Co Lodi), 1978

Oonbou's Foolish Pleasure, UDT (by Ch. Lynhaven's Timmy Taco O'El Toro out of Ch. Oonbou's Aruma Royal Muffin), 1983

Oonbou's Royal Dozier Dokein, CDXT (by Ch. Weeblu's Blaze of Joy out of Ch. Oonbou's Aruma Royal Muffin), 1987

Single copies of the AKC's *Obedience Regulations* may be obtained free by writing to them. Also available on request is their *Guidelines for Obedience Judges,* which has much valuable information for a better understanding of what judges are required to do and what they are looking for in both the dog's and handler's performance.

15

Register of Merit

THE SILKY TERRIER CLUB of America honors Silky Terriers that are sires and dams of numerous champions. Although the accurate worth of any sire or dam would be based on the percentage of champions produced from his or her offspring, such figures are not always available. This fact is not meant to diminish the value of the awards.

The Register of Merit system adopted by the club is based solely on the number of champions produced. It was implemented in 1983 and titles were awarded retroactive to 1959 to include all those qualifying since the breed was recognized by the American Kennel Club.

The Register of Merit (ROM) and Register of Merit Excellent (ROMX) titles are awarded annually by the club, and certificates are issued for those Silky Terriers owned by club members. Dogs must be sires of ten champions to qualify for the ROM title, and twenty champions are required for the ROMX title. For dams, the ROM title requires four champions and the ROMX title requires eight. The requirements were determined based on data supplied by the American Kennel Club's published records from 1959 through 1982. Based on these records, 7 percent of the champion-producing sires and 8 percent of the champion-producing dams became eligible for the Register of Merit titles.

Acquiring either of these titles is a noteworthy achievement. As of 1989 the Register of Merit title had been gained by 35 sires and 117 dams. Only 13 Silky Terrier sires and 15 dams had been awarded the Register of Merit Excellent title.

Ch. Silkallure Casanova is, without a doubt, the top Silky Terrier sire in the history of the breed, with 98 American champions and 3 international champions in Europe. Nearest to this record is Ch. Aslett's Kiku's Blue Streaker, sire of 53 American champions.

Among the Register of Merit Excellent dams, special recognition must be given to Verna Tucker's Ch. Fawn Hill Sweet Rosie O'Grady. She produced 16 champions—twice the required number for the title.

BRENHILL SPLINTERS
Whelped in Australia April 21, 1951.
Dam of four champions, granddam of twenty champions.
Breeder: Mrs. M. J. Brennan. Owner: Peggy Smith.

ARALUEN WINKY
DENNY BOY
AUS. CH. MISS DOLLY
PRISHWOOD SIR TEDDY
KENWYN
TINY SONJI
SONJI

PINTO
AUS. CH. ELLWYN GOLD PRINCE
ELLWYN GOLD LASSIE
ELLWYN LADY JUDY
DANIEL
PRINCESS JUDY
ECKRAL LADY JEAN

CH. WEXFORD POGO
Whelped in Australia June 14, 1952.
Sire of 15 champions, grandsire of 81 champions.
Breeder: Mrs. M. J. Brennan. Owner: Peggy Smith.

          PINTO
      AUS. CH. ELLWYN GOLD PRINCE
          ELLWYN GOLD LASSIE
BAULKHAM ROYAL JOHN
          AUS. CH. NIOBE GLOAMING BOY
      LADY PATSY
          AUS. CH. LADY MOLLY

          AUS. CH. NEWTOWN HARD TO BEAT
      NIOBE TIM
          AUS. CH. MISS LASSIE
ELOUERA JOY
          AUS. CH. NIOBE BOXER
      TECOONA TESSIE
          TECOONA PATSY

AUS. CH. KELSO LADY SUSAN
Whelped in Australia May 4, 1953. Dam of one champion, granddam
of 27 champions. Breeder: Kelso Kennels. Owner: Robert Cooley.

JOLLY PRINCE OF LITHGOW
AUS. CH. SILVER PRINCE OF LITHGOW
CLARA OF LITHGOW
KELSO BEAU IDEAL
AUS. CH. SPARKLING SIR TITCH
AUS. CH. SPARKLING PRINCESS ARMLEY
AUS. CH. LADY ARMLEY

SILVER STAR OF KELSO
LUCKY STAR OF KELSO
MISS JUDY OF DEANDALE
MIRANDA OF KELSO
AUS. CH. TEDDY OF HILLSIDE
LADY PAM OF HILLSIDE
JUDY OF HILLSIDE

AUS. CH. BOWENVALE MURRAY
Whelped in Australia May 25, 1955. Sire of one champion, grandsire of 30 champions. Breeder: Bowenvale Kennels. Owner: Robert Cooley.

                ROFTER JAMES
          ROFTER TEXAS
                MISS BONNIE OF DEANDALE
GWENALRE BOBBIE
                ROFTER TEXAS
          GWENALRE JENNY
                BEN LOCIN BONNIE

                ROFTER TEXAS
          GWENALRE BOBBIE
                GWENALRE JENNIE
AUS. CH. RIAWENA LINDY LOU
                ROFTER TEXAS
          LEVENA PIXY MASON
                LADY LYNETTE

PHOTO NOT AVAILABLE

CH. COOLAROO SIR WINSTON, ROMX Sire
Whelped January 31, 1958.
Breeder: Robert Cooley. Owners: Susan and Fred Stern.

ROFTER TEXAS
GWENALRE BOBBIE
GWENALRE JENNY
AUS. CH. BOWENVALE MURRAY (Import)
GWENALRE BOBBIE
AUS. CH. RIAWENA LINDY LOU
LEVENA PIXY MASON

AUS. CH. SILVER PRINCE OF LITHGOW
KELSO BEAU IDEAL
AUS. CH. SPARKLING PRINCESS ARMLEY
AUS. CH. KELSO LADY SUSAN (Import)
LUCKY STAR OF KELSO
MIRANDA OF KELSO
LADY PAM OF HILLSIDE

CH. REDWAY BUSTER, ROMX Sire
Whelped April 17, 1962.
Breeder: Peggy Smith. Owner: Beverly Lehnig.

AUS. CH. ELLWYN GOLD PRINCE
BAULKHAM ROYAL JOHN
LADY PATSY
CH. WEXFORD POGO (Import)
NIOBE TIM
ELOUERA JOY
TECOONA TESSIE

BAULKHAM ROYAL JOHN
CH. WEXFORD POGO (Import)
ELOUERA JOY
REDWAY SMITH'S GAMBLE
PRISHWOOD SIR TEDDY
BRENHILL SPLINTERS (Import)
ELLWYN LADY JUDY

CH. SILKALLURE CASANOVA, ROMX Sire
Whelped January 28, 1964.
Breeder-owners: Victor and Mona Bracco.

> GWENALRE BOBBIE
>> AUS. CH. BOWENVALE MURRAY (Import)
> AUS. CH. RIAWENA LINDY LOU
>>> CH. COOLAROO SIR WINSTON
> KELSO BEAU IDEAL
>> AUS. CH. KELSO LADY SUSAN (Import)
> MIRANDA OF KELSO
>
> SMITHFIELD MAX
>> AUS. CH. PRAIRIE PLAYBOY (Import)
> PRAIRIE GYPSY
>>> BONDOON'S SILKIE SULLIVAN
> AUS. CH. ALDOON PETE
>> PETEENA BONNIE (Import)
> AUS. CH. ELLWYN LADY SUSAN

CH. SILTI'S JOY BOY, ROMX Sire
Whelped May 15, 1968.
Breeder-owner: Mary T. Estrin.

CH. WEXFORD POGO (Import)
CH. REDWAY BEAU BRUMMELL
BRENHILL SPLINTERS (Import)
CH. CLAVONS BLUE RAIN
KANIMBLA SIR POTCH
KANIMBLA LADY PENELOPE
KANIMBLA FATIMA

CH. COOLAROO SIR WINSTON
COOLAROO LORD ARBIE
CH. MILAN BABS (Import)
CH. COOLAROO DAME WINTIKI
AUS. CH. BOWENVALE MURRAY (Import)
COOLAROO MISS SUSIE
YOORALLA PATSY ANNE (Import)

CH. CASA DE CASEYS ADMIRAL NELSON, ROMX Sire
Whelped May 3, 1969.
Breeders: Victor and Mona Bracco. Owner: Marie Nelson.

AUS. CH. BOWENVALE MURRAY (Import)
CH. COOLAROO SIR WINSTON
AUS. CH. KELSO LADY SUSAN (Import)
CH. SILKALLURE CASANOVA
AUS. CH. PRAIRIE PLAYBOY (Import)
BONDOON'S SILKIE SULLIVAN
PETEENA BONNIE (Import)

AUS. CH. KOOLAMINA SANTE
AUS. CH. LYLAC PLAYBOY
AUS. CH. LYLAC THELLY
EILART SHADEE LADY (Import)
AUS. CH. LYLAC PLAYBOY
AUS. CH. EILART GAY LINDY
AUS. CH. GAYDELL MITZI

CH. ROYALINE DON JUAN OF CASANOVA, ROMX Sire
Whelped January 8, 1970.
Breeders: Victor and Mona Bracco. Owners: Robert and Gloria Farron.

            AUS. CH. BOWENVALE MURRAY (Import)
       CH. COOLAROO SIR WINSTON
            AUS. CH. KELSO LADY SUSAN (Import)
CH. SILKALLURE CASANOVA
            AUS. CH. PRAIRIE PLAYBOY (Import)
       BONDOON'S SILKIE SULLIVAN
            PETEENA BONNIE (Import)

            AUS. CH. KOOLAMINA SANTE
       AUS. CH. LYLAC PLAYBOY
            AUS. CH. LYLAC THELLY
EILART SHADEE LADY (Import)
            AUS. CH. LYLAC PLAYBOY
       AUS. CH. EILART GAY LINDY
            AUS. CH. GAYDELL MITZI

CH. WEEBLU'S BLAZE OF JOY, ROMX Sire
Whelped March 19, 1973.
Breeder-owner: Florence Males.

CH. REDWAY BEAU BRUMMELL
CH. CLAVONS BLUE RAIN
KANIMBLA LADY PENELOPE
CH. SILTI'S JOY BOY
COOLAROO LORD ARBIE
CH. COOLAROO DAME WINTIKI
COOLAROO MISS SUSIE

CH. SILKALLURE REXANDY
CH. SILKALLURE REXANTHONY
WINSTON'S CINDERELLA
CH. SILKALLURE WEE ONE
CH. SILKALLURE WINANDY
SILKALLURE SMALL WONDER
SILKALLURE EVENING STAR

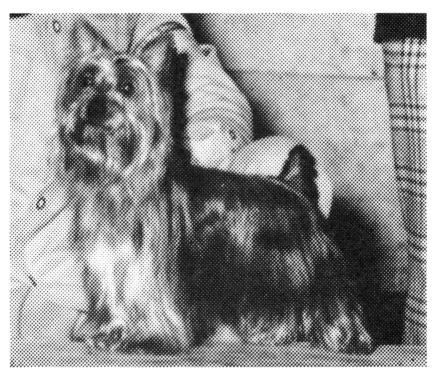

CH. ASLETT'S KIKU'S BLUE STREAKER, ROMX Sire
Whelped June 19, 1975.
Breeders: Janet Aslett and Kay Magnussen. Owners: Kay and Jon
Magnussen.

CH. REDWAY LORD MICHAEL
CH. WILHAVEN'S WEE SWEET WILLIAM
CH. WILHAVEN'S WEE DAISY
CH. HARGILL'S JOLLY JAMBOREE
CH. REDWAY BUSTER
CH. REBEL DANCING ANGEL
REBEL APRIL ANGEL

CH. HARGILL'S JOLLY JAMBOREE
CH. HARGILL'S PETER'S PAL SO FANCY
CH. NORGE WESTRALIAN FANCY (Import)
CH. KIKU'S ST. NICKS VIXEN
CH. MAVROB SMOKEE
CH. WYM WEY WITH A WAG
CH. KADINA OF CARRIEWERLOO

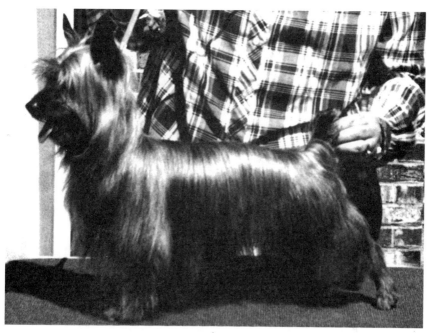

CH. ADMIRAL'S CASANOVA, ROMX Sire
Whelped June 9, 1977.
Breeder-owner: Anne Edgar.

AUS. CH. BOWENVALE MURRAY (Import)
CH. COOLAROO SIR WINSTON
AUS. CH. KELSO LADY SUSAN (Import)
CH. SILKALLURE CASANOVA
AUS. CH. PRAIRIE PLAYBOY (Import)
BONDOON'S SILKIE SULLIVAN
PETEENA BONNIE (Import)

CH. SILKALLURE CASANOVA
CH. CASA DE CASEY TOUCH OF CLASS
EILART SHADEE LADY (Import)
CH. ADMIRAL'S CLASSY LASSIE
CH. CASA DE CASEY'S MY GUY
ADMIRAL'S DELPHINIUM
TUPPENCE

TAK'OPE TU-SHU, ROMX Sire
Whelped February 18, 1978.
Breeder: Mrs. Jack Haley. Owner: Pam Laperruque.

KOONOONA DANNIE
CH. KOONOONA NODDI (Import)
SILVERDIN UP AND AWAY
CH. MIDLAND KOONOONA NODDI TOO
CH. KOONOONA BO BO (Import)
CH. MIDLAND'S KOONOONA MATILDA
CH. LYLAC JAN (Import)

CH. HARGILL'S PETER'S PAL SO FANCY
CH. HARGILL'S GUY'S GEMINI
CH. HARGILL'S SHARI O'SILKALLURE
CH. TAK'OPE CANBERRA MISTI DAWN
CH. HARGILL'S PETER'S PAL SO FANCY
CH. HARGILL'S GUY'S GINA BLAE JOIA
CH. REBEL DANCING ANGEL

CH. RITA'S FIREBRAND OF FAWN HILL, ROMX Sire
Whelped July 3, 1978.
Breeder: Rita Dawson. Owners: Verna Tucker and Elizabeth Click.

CH. ROYALINE DON JUAN OF CASANOVA
CH. NOWIFL'S BEST O'LUCK
CH. FAWN HILL THE LUCKY SPOT
CH. FAWN HILL THE DONNYBROOK
CH. LANALLUNGA LORD TIMOTHY
FAWN HILL ROXANNE
FAWN HILL SMALL WANDA

CH. KIKU'S J.J. JAMBOREE C.D.
CH. KIKU'S BIT O'TUFF STUFF
WEE BONNIE MISSY MILAN
CH. KIKU'S RITA'S APRIL ABIGAIL
D'UNDER AVANBLU CHIP STAMPER
HEFNER'S BARBI BENTON O'D'UNDER
D'UNDER PLAYBOY CENTERFOLD

CH. WEEBLU'S TRAILBLAZER OF DON-EL, ROMX Sire
Whelped April 22, 1979.
Breeders: Don and Helen Thompson. Owner: Florence A. Males.

CH. CLAVONS BLUE RAIN
CH. SILTI'S JOY BOY
CH. COOLAROO DAME WINTIKI
CH. WEEBLU'S BLAZE OF JOY
CH. SILKALLURE REXANTHONY
CH. SILKALLURE WEE ONE
SILKALLURE SMALL WONDER

CH. BONNEEN'S ARUNTA CHIEFTAIN
CH. LU-JON'S LORD CAGNEY OF TUNNEY
BRANDY OF TUNNEY
CH. DON-EL'S TOO GOOD TO BE TRUE
CH. SILKALLURE CASANOVA
CH. DON-EL'S LOOK OF ELEGANCE
PRINCESS PARIZADE

CH. MARINA'S DALLAS, ROMX Sire
Whelped October 18, 1980.
Breeders: Joene Kelly and Laurie Ericson. Owners: Dr. and Mrs. Barry Kelly.

<pre>
                    CH. CLAVONS BLUE RAIN
          CH. SILTI'S JOY BOY
                    CH. COOLAROO DAME WINTIKI
CH. WEEBLU'S BLAZE OF JOY
                    CH. SILKALLURE REXANTHONY
          CH. SILKALLURE WEE ONE
                    SILKALLURE SMALL WONDER

                    CH. HARGILL'S JOLLY JAMBOREE
          CH. ASLETT'S KIKU'S BLUE STREAKER
                    CH. KIKU'S ST. NICKS VIXEN
CH. KIKU'S MARINA'S WHIMSEY
                    CH. ROYALINE DON JUAN OF CASANOVA
          ROYALINE CHELSEA MORNING
                    ROYALINE REGINA CASA DE CASEY
</pre>

CH. ALDOON LADY MARRIE, ROMX Dam (Import)
Whelped July 20, 1960.
Breeder: Mrs. J. Milne. Owner: Mildred Pequignot.

AUS. CH. TIBET RADIANT FLASH
VERNENA MICKY
TIBET WHISPERING HOPE
AUS. CH. ALDOON SIVAM
WINSOME BEAU IDEAL
ALDOON SUSIE
AUS. CH. ALDOON TRIXIE

AUS. CH. ELLWYN GOLD COBBY
AUS. CH. ALDOON PRINCE
ALDOON BETSY
ALDOON LASSIE
DANIEL
ECKRAL LADY MYRTLE
ECKRAL LADY BOBS

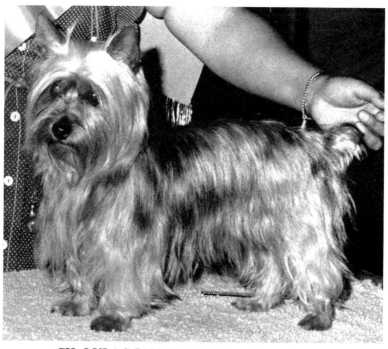

CH. LYLAC JAN, ROMX Dam (Import)
Whelped June 29, 1962.
Breeder: Nancy Glynn. Owner: Carmen Cananzi.

AUS. CH. BOWENVALE PRINCE ROBBIE
AUS. CH. HATFIELD MASTER REX
VANESTA PETIT CHERI
LEROY MISTY
AUS. CH. MIAMI GOLD FLASH
LYLAC RHONDA
PRAIRIE DOROTHY

AUS. CH. ELLWYN GOLD COBBY
AUS. CH. ALDOON PRINCE
ALDOON BETSY
ALDOON WENDY ANN
AUS. CH. ELLWYN GOLD GEM
GLENBOIG JEAN
ECKRAL LADY JEAN

EILART SHADEE LADY, ROMX Dam (Import)
Whelped September 19, 1967.
Breeder: A. E. and Mrs. Huthnance. Owners: Victor and Mona Bracco.

AUS. CH. PRAIRIE PLAYBOY
AUS. CH. KOOLAMINA SANTE
KOOLAMINA GAY GIRL
AUS. CH. LYLAC PLAYBOY
AUS. CH. STROUD SMILING SMITTY
AUS. CH. LYLAC THELLY
LYLAC PENNY

AUS. CH. KOOLAMINA SANTE
AUS. CH. LYLAC PLAYBOY
AUS. CH. LYLAC THELLY
AUS. CH. EILART GAY LINDY
AUS. CH. BOUDEN BEAU
AUS. CH. GAYDELL MITZI
ALDOON TANYA

CH. HARGILL'S OLIVER'S OLIVIA, ROMX Dam
Whelped March 19, 1971.
Breeder: Harriet Gill. Owners: Arlene Steinle and Diane Fenger.

CH. HARGILL'S JOLLY JAMBOREE
CH. HARGILL'S PETER'S PAL SO FANCY
CH. NORGE WESTRALIAN FANCY (Import)
CH. HARGILL'S GUYS GEMINI
CH. SILKALLURE PRINCE CHARMING
CH. HARGILL'S SHARI O'SILKALLURE
CH. REBEL DANCING ANGEL

AUS. CH. NORGE EL RAJAH II
NORGE EL RANGER II
NORGE SELECTED LADY
CH. NORGE WESTRALIAN FANCY (Import)
SWALEDALE SANTE FE
AUS. CH. NORGE EVENING STAR
GLEN ELSA MITZIE

CH. SILKALLURE WEE ONE, ROMX Dam
Whelped January 23, 1971.
Breeders: B. E. and J. Claybrook. Owner: Florence Males.

```
          CH. COOLAROO SIR WINSTON
      CH. SILKALLURE REXANDY
          CH. SILKALLURE REXANNE (Import in utero)
CH. SILKALLURE REXANTHONY
          CH. COOLAROO SIR WINSTON
      WINSTON'S CINDERELLA
          COOLAROO'S CINDERELLA

          CH. SILKALLURE REXANDY
      CH. SILKALLURE WINANDY
          BONDOON'S SILKIE SULLIVAN
SILKALLURE SMALL WONDER
          CH. COOLAROO SIR WINSTON
      SILKALLURE EVENING STAR
          CH. SILKALLURE REXALINDA
```

CH. KOALA MISS FANCY CASA DE CASEY, ROMX Dam
Whelped March 10, 1972.
Breeders: Victor and Mona Bracco. Owners: Doreen and Jason Gross.

AUS. CH. BOWENVALE MURRAY (Import)
CH. COOLAROO SIR WINSTON
AUS. CH. KELSO LADY SUSAN (Import)
CH. SILKALLURE CASANOVA
AUS. CH. PRAIRIE PLAYBOY (Import)
BONDOON'S SILKIE SULLIVAN
PETEENA BONNIE (Import)

LAUROSA PRINCE ANTON
LAUROSA PERRY
TAMWORTH JOY BELLE
LAUROSA TRACY BELLE (Import)
PERRYWINKLE NICKY
BAYUDA GAY LADY
YOORALLA PINKY

CH. EASTON'S BLUEBERRY MUFFIN, ROMX Dam
Whelped August 25, 1974.
Breeder: Robert Easton. Owners: Mr. and Mrs. Robert Easton.

CH. HARGILL'S JOLLY JAMBOREE
CH. KI KU'S J.J. JAMBOREE C.D.
CH. WYM WEY WITH A WAG
CH. KIKU'S BIT O'TUFF STUFF
MUNBILLA ANZAC LAD (Import)
WEE BONNIE MISSY MILAN
SINSPARK JULIES GEM (Import)

CH. COOLAROO SIR WINSTON
SILKALLURE WINSTON'S IMAGE
HILLSIDE LADY COLLEEN (Import)
TINA MARANN
COOLAROO LORD ARBIE
PASSIONATE SERENA MARANN
COOLAROO PRINCESS BLUE BELL

CH. ADMIRAL'S CLASSY LASSIE, ROMX Dam
Whelped January 18, 1975.
Breeders: Anne Edgar and J. K. Kampf. Owner: Anne Edgar.

CH. COOLAROO SIR WINSTON
CH. SILKALLURE CASANOVA
BONDOON'S SILKIE SULLIVAN
CH. CASA DE CASEY TOUCH OF CLASS
AUS. CH. LYLAC PLAYBOY
EILART SHADEE LADY (Import)
AUS. CH. EILART GAY LINDY

CH. SILKALLURE CASANOVA
CH. CASA DE CASEY'S MY GUY
LAUROSA STAR BUTIBEL (Import)
ADMIRAL'S DELPHINIUM
AUS. CH. BONNEEN PHILIP (Import)
TUPPENCE
COOLAROO LADY KARRIE

CH. KIRSTIN'S KASSE OF CASANOVA, ROMX Dam
Whelped August 5, 1976.
Breeders: D. F. and P. A. Siemer. Owners: Kirstin and Kris Griffin.

TAMWORTH STAR RICKY (Import)
COOLAROO LORD MONTGOMERY III
HILLCREST WEE MAGGIE
CH. SHANIS KOALA SPORT
CH. SILKALLURE CASANOVA
CH. SHANIS LA CONTESSA DU CASEY
CH. COOLAROO PRINCESS SHANI

CH. COOLAROO SIR WINSTON
CH. SILKALLURE CASANOVA
BONDOON'S SILKIE SULLIVAN
CH. RONCO'S CASSANDRA OF CASANOVA
CH. SILKALLURE CASANOVA
CH. CASA DE CASEY'S DESTINY'S TOT
SILKALLURE BRIGADOON

CH. AVONWYCK COUNTRY COUNTESS, ROMX Dam
Whelped October 15, 1976.
Breeder: Janean Wylie. Owners: Janean Wylie and Mrs. E. L. Macy.

AUS. CH. KOOLAMINA SANTE
AUS. CH. LYLAC PLAYBOY
AUS. CH. LYLAC THELLEY
CH. LYLAC BLUE PRINCE (Import)
PRAIRIE SIR JAMES
PRAIRIE DAIL
LYLAC PANSY

CH. REDWAY BUSTER
CH. REBEL PETER PIPER
REBEL APRIL ANGEL
CH. AVONWYCK CALL ME KINDRA
CH. SILKALLURE CASANOVA
CH. AVONWYCK MAIRI STUART
MAVROB FAIR TRINA, CD

CH. FAWN HILL SWEET ROSIE O'GRADY, ROMX Dam
Whelped May 8, 1977.
Breeders: Verna Tucker and Eleanor Norton. Owner: Verna Tucker.

CH. ROYALINE DON JUAN OF CASANOVA
CH. NOWIFL'S BEST O'LUCK
CH. FAWN HILL THE LUCKY SPOT
CH. FAWN HILL THE DONNYBROOK
CH. LANALLUNGA LORD TIMOTHY
FAWN HILL ROXANNE
FAWN HILL SMALL WANDA

CH. FAWN HILL THE SOROBAN
FAWN HILL THE SOJOURNER
REDWAY WEXFORD WIND SONG
FAWN HILL THE GINGEROO
CH. FAWN HILL THE SOROBAN
GINGEROO'S GAY BONNIE BLUE
GINGEROO'S GAY GIRL

CH. WOODLYNND'S HECATE, ROMX Dam
Whelped October 24, 1978.
Breeders: Les and Sandra Baxter. Owner: M. Louise Coviello.

CH. HARGILL'S JOLLY JAMBOREE
CH. ASLETT'S KIKU'S BLUE STREAKER
CH. KIKU'S ST. NICKS VIXEN
CH. KIKU'S WINALOT WILLIE
CH. KIKU'S BIT O'TUFF STUFF
CH. KIKU'S BIT O'KANDY LUV
CH. HARGILL'S KIKU'S KANDY KISSES

CH. FAWN HILL ROUSTABOUT
WOODLYNND CASANOVA CREEK RUN
LADY MUFFIN
WOODLYNNDS WEE JULEE
BUSTER BLUE
WOODLYNNDS TIFANY O'CREEK RUN
BRINKERHOFF'S LOVABLE LEILA

CH. AUSTRAL JENOLAN OUR GAL SAL, ROMX Dam
Whelped January 4, 1979.
Breeders: Arlene Lewis and Mildred Pequignot. Owner: William Deller.

HAYES' JUNIOR DE LA EK
CH. GEM-G'S KOOL HAND LUKE
HAYES' LADY TINA DE LA KREAUX
CH. SILKALLURE ARROGANT ARGUS
CH. SILKALLURE REXANDY
CH. KRISKAH MISTE OF REXANDY
NIGHT MIST OF THE VALLEY

AUS. CH. LYLAC PLAYBOY
CH. LYLAC BLUE PRINCE (Import)
PRAIRIE DAIL
CH. JENOLAN AUSTRAL SATIN TASSEL
CH. SILKALLURE SIR WINKAH
CH. BLU-N-TAN GODDESS PANDORA
AUSSIE'S SILKALLURE GODDESS

CH. FAWN HILL'S JESSAMYN AT LUXA, CD, ROMX Dam
Whelped July 10, 1979.
Breeder: Verna Tucker. Owner: Susan O'Rear.

CH. NOWIFL'S BEST O'LUCK
CH. FAWN HILL THE DONNYBROOK
FAWN HILL ROXANNE
CH. RITA'S FIREBRAND OF FAWN HILL
CH. KIKU'S BIT O'TUFF STUFF
CH. KIKU'S RITA'S APRIL ABIGAIL
HEFNER'S BARBI BENTON O'D'UNDER

CH. NOWIFL'S BEST O'LUCK
CH. FAWN HILL THE DONNYBROOK
FAWN HILL ROXANNE
CH. FAWN HILL SWEET ROSIE O'GRADY
FAWN HILL THE SOJOURNER
FAWN HILL THE GINGEROO
CH. GINGEROO'S GAY BONNIE BLUE

CH. AUSTRAL MISTIBLU HEATHER, ROMX Dam
Whelped October 25, 1980.
Breeder-owner: William Deller.

CH. SILKALLURE ARROGANT ARGUS
CH. JENOLAN AUSTRAL DOHUGAMIEH
CH. JENOLAN SUGAR COOKIE AUSTRAL
CH. AUSTRAL BLUE BEAU JANGLES
CH. LYLAC BLUE PRINCE (Import)
CH. JENOLAN AUSTRAL SATIN TASSEL
CH. BLU-N-TAN GODDESS PANDORA

CH. GEM-G'S KOOL HAND LUKE
CH. SILKALLURE ARROGANT ARGUS
CH. KRISKAH MISTE OF REXANDY
CH. AUSTRAL JENOLAN OUR GAL SAL
CH. LYLAC BLUE PRINCE (Import)
CH. JENOLAN AUSTRAL SATIN TASSEL
CH. BLU-N-TAN GODDESS PANDORA

16

The Silky Terrier Clubs

On MARCH 25, 1955, a small group of enthusiastic Silky Terrier fanciers living in the San Francisco Bay area met in Richmond, California, at the home of Roland and Betty Stegeman. At this meeting they founded the Sydney Silky Terrier Club of America. Their goal was to work toward gaining full American Kennel Club recognition for the breed, thereby making it eligible to compete for championship points.

The ten people who met that day were Vivien Chamberlain, Margaret Citrino, Florence Dahlstrom, Thomas Fromm, Robert Garrett, Howard Jensen, Mrs. A. H. Nelson, Doris Roesling and Roland and Betty Stegeman, the founding members of the club. Within a short time club membership had climbed to forty-nine; these were the charter members of the club. In 1978 the four remaining charter members were made life members. They were Florence Dahlstrom, Howard Jensen, Josephine Seligman and Peggy Smith.

In July 1955 the club members voted to conform to the AKC's preferred name, Silky Terriers, as they were classified in the Miscellaneous class at shows. The "Sydney" was dropped from the name and the club became known as the Silky Terrier Club of America.

In 1956 the author was serving as president and recording secretary of the club and set up the club's Stud Book. Sires, dams, and their offspring were recorded in it and registered with the Silky Terrier Club of America; in turn, the club registered each with the Royal Agriculture Society Kennel Club in Sydney, Australia. In order to do this each American breeder had to choose a kennel prefix, which was then registered in Australia by the Silky Terrier Club of America.

More and more Silkys were being shown in the Miscellaneous classes nationwide, and by 1958 more than four hundred Silkys had been registered with the Silky Terrier Club of America. At this point, the club formally requested full recognition of the breed from the AKC.

In June 1958 the AKC advised the club that they were preparing special registration application forms for Silky Terriers. These were mailed by the club to all owners whose Silkys were registered with the club.

On March 30, 1959, the club's Stud Book was sent to the AKC along with 440 registration applications, each accompanied by a photograph of the dog and a six-generation pedigree. On May 9, 1959, Silky Terriers were accepted by the AKC as the 113th breed to be eligible to compete for championship points.

The club's next goal was to hold Sanctioned Matches, which were necessary to qualify for Specialty shows for the breed. The AKC did not require the club to hold Sanctioned B Matches but approved a Sanctioned A Match for August 13, 1960, in Los Altos Hills, California. Eight months later, on April 23, 1961, the second Sanctioned A Match took place at the same location. Both were termed "qualifying Matches" by the AKC.

The first Silky Terrier Club of America Specialty show was held November 19, 1961, in conjunction with the San Mateo Kennel Club's show in California. One National Specialty was held yearly until 1968.

Beginning in 1968 two National Specialties were held yearly—one in the East, the other in the West. The majority of eastern fanciers attended only the eastern Specialty, with the same results in the West. In 1974, to encourage more national participation, the club returned to holding only one Specialty each year in different zones throughout the country. These National Specialties now have entries from all across the country and Canada. Since 1985, entries have been well over the one hundred mark.

Am. and Can. Ch. Tessier Danielle of Shoshana (by Ch. Silwynd Apricot Cordial out of Ch. Kiku's Vivacious Vonda), a Specialty Best of Opposite Sex winner. Bred by Kay Magnussen and Sandy Mesmer and owned by Susan Mezistrano and Jon Magnussen. *Bill Francis*

The next step was to become a member club of the AKC, which would permit delegate representation at the AKC's quarterly meetings in New York. The Silky Terrier Club of America's initial membership application was denied on the grounds that the vast majority of members lived in California. In the AKC's opinion the club was not representing the breed nationally. As a result of the turndown a comprehensive report was submitted to the AKC that proved to its satisfaction that the club was representing the majority of breeders and exhibitors throughout the country. The club was accepted as a member club of the AKC in 1966. California memberships still greatly outnumber those in other states. The Silky Terrier Club of America's 1989 membership roster of more than 400 showed ninety-one living in California; the next highest number was twenty-nine in Texas.

Dr. Benjamin Ackerman served as the club's first delegate. Mrs. Benjamin (Edna) Ackerman is now serving in that capacity. She is an AKC judge and was a breeder and exhibitor of top-quality Silky Terriers.

The club's monthly publication is the *Silky Terrier Club of America Newsletter*. It was inaugurated in March 1955 by Howard Jensen, the first editor. Since then the editors have been Shirley Cahill, Elinor Morrison, Jean Gonzales, Betty Young, Peggy Smith, Phyllis Cook, Connie Alber, Arlene Lewis, Irma Marshall, Louise Coviello and Kathy Hughes. Special recognition must be given to Arlene Lewis for her ten years as editor.

Also deserving special recognition are Betty Britt and Laurel Gilbertson, who have continued to serve the club in many important capacities ever since becoming members in 1957.

Since 1980 a club yearbook has been published, edited by Eleanor Norton and Arlene Lewis. Among other items of interest, the yearbook contains pedigrees of all the previous year's new champions and Obedience title holders, with the majority of them pictured.

Many have contributed their expertise and time to the club. As president: Margaret Citrino, Peggy Smith, Rinaldo Navarro, Frances Van Etten, Laurel Gilbertson, Maurice Poimiroo, Frank Abarta, James Young, Dorothy Hicks, Connie Alber, Richard Estrin, Harry Eastham, Louise Rosewell, Eleanor Norton, Beverly Lehnig and Patricia Walton. As recording and/or corresponding secretary: Robert Garrett, Howard Jensen, Peggy Smith, Jan Cohen, Betty Britt, Dolly Navarro, Arline Clark, Don Thompson, Louise

High in Trial at the 1980 Silky Terrier Club of America Specialty went to Ch. Tails West Tammy, UD, bred by Aleida Castetter and owned by Dorothy Huber.

Rosewell, Arlene Byers, Eleanor Norton, Beverly Lehnig and Florence Males. As treasurer: Florence Dahlstrom, Paul Hefner, Silvana Ghiozzi, Peggy Lawson, Dawn Slowi and Lee Easton.

Many volunteers have served the club well as members of the board of directors and in other capacities.

REGIONAL CLUBS

The City of Angels Silky Terrier Club, in the Los Angeles area of California, is the only regional club eligible to hold Specialty shows. Yearly shows have been held by this group since 1973.

The Silky Terrier Club of Northern California, organized in 1981, held fun matches twice yearly until 1988, when they were approved by the AKC to hold Sanctioned B Matches. Their goal is to hold Specialty shows in the San Francisco Bay Area.

The Greater Milwaukee Silky Terrier Club, which was spearheaded by Phyllis Cook, is no longer in existence. Eight yearly Specialties were held by this club from 1973 to 1980. Unfortunately, the number of exhibitors and breeders in the area dropped off, causing it to be impractical for the club to continue.

Addresses for the Silky Terrier Club of America, the City of Angels Silky Terrier Club and the Silky Terrier Club of Northern California may be obtained by written request to the American Kennel Club.

APPENDIX

Competing in American Kennel Club Shows

M̲ORE THAN ONE THOUSAND all-breed dog shows, sanctioned by the American Kennel Club, are held annually in the United States. Dogs must be entered in these shows well in advance. Entries for most have to be made at least three weeks prior to the date of the show. Dogs are required to be six months of age to be eligible for entry.

The majority of all-breed kennel clubs employ superintendents or secretaries to handle the entries for their shows. You can contact your local all-breed kennel club for the address of their superintendent or secretary. Entry forms can be obtained from them by written request. Along with the entry form you will receive information about the show in a packet called a Premium List. This contains details concerning the show, including the classes available for your dog's entry.

The reverse side of the entry form, for AKC shows, states, in part: "I acknowledge that the *Rules Applying to Registration and Dog Shows* and, if this entry is for an obedience trial, the *Obedience Regulations,* have been made available to me, and that I am familiar with their contents." When you sign the entry blank you agree to abide by the rules and regulations of the AKC. A free copy of both pamphlets can be obtained from the AKC upon request.

After obtaining an entry form you must decide in which class you will enter your dog. It is advisable to enter only one class, even though your dog may be eligible for more than one. Additional details concerning eligibility for entry in the classes should be carefully checked in the rule pamphlets.

The following are brief explanations of the Conformation classes. Conformation judging is based on how the physical attributes of individual dogs comply with the AKC's Standard for their breed.

The Puppy class is for dogs that are six months of age but under twelve months. Some shows divide this class—one for dogs six months but under nine months and another for nine months but under twelve months. This will be indicated in the Premium List.

The Novice class is for dogs that are six months of age and over that have not won three first prizes in this class or a first prize in the Bred-by-Exhibitor, American-bred, or Open class, nor any points toward their championships. Novice class entries must have been whelped in the United States, Canada or Mexico.

The Bred-by-Exhibitor class entries must be handled in this class by the breeder or by a member of his or her immediate family.

The American-bred class is for dogs whelped in the United States from a mating that took place there.

The Open class is so named because it is "open to all" dogs six months of age or over.

It is not possible to pre-enter the Winners class. Entry in this class is gained by taking a first prize in one of the previous classes. The winner of first place in each of the classes, if not defeated in another class, goes back into the ring to compete for Winners Dog or Winners Bitch. If your dog takes second place you should remain at ringside on stand-by. If the dog that took first place in your dog's class is chosen as Winners Dog or Winners Bitch, your dog must go back into the ring to compete for Reserve Winners with the remaining first-place dogs. If, for some reason, the AKC declares the Winners Dog or Bitch to be ineligible for this award, the Reserve winner becomes the Winners Dog or Bitch.

OFFICIAL AMERICAN KENNEL CLUB ENTRY FORM

SAMPLE

I ENCLOSE $ . . . . for entry fees

IMPORTANT—Read Carefully Instructions on Reverse Side Before Filling Out. Numbers in the boxes indicate sections of the instructions relevant to the information needed in that box (PLEASE PRINT)

BREED	VARIETY [1]		SEX

DOG [2] [3] SHOW CLASS		CLASS ☐ DIVISION Weight color etc	
ADDITIONAL CLASSES	OBEDIENCE TRIAL CLASS	JR SHOWMANSHIP CLASS	

NAME OF (See Back)
JUNIOR HANDLER (if any)

FULL
NAME
OF DOG

Enter number here

☐ AKC REG NO
☐ AKC LITTER NO
☐ ILP NO
☐ FOREIGN REG NO & COUNTRY

DATE OF
BIRTH

PLACE OF ☐ USA   ☐ Canada   ☐ Foreign
BIRTH   Do not print the above in catalog

BREEDER

SIRE

DAM

ACTUAL OWNER(S) _____
[4]   (Please Print)
OWNER'S ADDRESS _____
CITY _____ STATE _____ ZIP _____

NAME OF OWNERS AGENT
(IF ANY) AT THE SHOW _____

I CERTIFY that I am the actual owner of the dog, or that I am the duly authorized agent of the actual owner whose name I have entered above. In consideration of the acceptance of this entry, I (we) agree to abide by the rules and regulations of The American Kennel Club in effect at the time of this show or obedience trial, and by any additional rules and regulations appearing in the premium list for this show or obedience trial or both, and further agree to be bound by the "Agreement" printed on the reverse side of this entry form. I (we) certify and represent that the dog entered is not a hazard to persons or other dogs. This entry is submitted for acceptance on the foregoing representation and agreement

SIGNATURE of owner or his agent
duly authorized to make this entry _____
TELEPHONE # _____

A sample entry form.

Best Toy Brace in Show at the 75th anniversary show of the Golden Gate Kennel Club in 1985: Ch. Weeblu's Blazing Tiara and Ch. Weeblu's Special Gift of Blaze, CD (by Ch. Weeblu's Blaze of Joy out of Ch. Weeblu's Puff 'N Joy's Delight), bred and owned by Florence Males.

Sixteen-year-old Kriste Griffin handled her Ch. Kirstin's Kasse of Cassanova to best of Opposite Sex at the 1979 Westminster Kennel Club show. Kasse is by Ch. Shanis Koala Sport out of Ch. Ronco's Cassandra of Casanova, bred by D. and P. Siemer. The judge was Joan Alexander. *Ashbey*

The Winners Dog and Winners Bitch are awarded a specified number of championship points (up to a maximum of five) if there are a sufficient number of dogs in competition. This is determined by the the AKC's Schedule of Points, and is published near the front of the catalog for each show. To become a champion, a dog or bitch must earn a total of fifteen points, including two wins of at least three points each. The fifteen points must be won under at least three judges.

Entry in the Best of Breed Class is limited to those dogs and bitches that have completed their championships. The Winners Dog and Winners Bitch also compete in this class for Best of Breed, and one of them is awarded Best of Winners. An award is also given for Best of Opposite Sex to the Best of Breed winner.

At all-breed shows the Best of Breed Silky Terrier goes on to compete in the Toy Group. If the Silky takes first place in this Group, it goes on to compete against the other six Group winners for the Best in Show award.

A Specialty show is one that is held for specified breeds. At a Silky Terrier Specialty show only Silky Terriers are entered. At Specialty shows there is one additional regular class that may be offered—the Twelve- to Eighteen-Month class—and additional classes that are not normally offered at all-breed shows. These are called nonregular classes, and they are the Veteran Dog class, the Veteran Bitch class, the Stud Dog class, the Brood Bitch class, the Brace class and the Team class.

Entries in the Veteran classes are usually required to be seven years of age or older. The winner of first place in each sex competes in the Best of Breed class, and it is not unusual for one of them to take the top award. It is also a chance to show off a dog you are extremely proud of that may never have been seen before by some of the exhibitors or spectators.

Best of Breed, Best of Opposite Sex and Best of Winners are chosen at Specialty shows in the same manner as they are at all-breed shows. An award that is available only at Specialty shows that are held apart from all-breed shows is Best Puppy in Show. The first-place winners of the four puppy classes compete for this honor.

The Stud Dog and Brood Bitch classes are for stud dogs and brood bitches and two or more of their offspring, as specified in the Premium List, which are also entered in other classes at the show. In the judging of this class, only the quality of the offspring is to be considered by the judge.

Best in Sweepstakes at the Silky Terrier Club of America Specialty show, July 1973, is soon to become Ch. Silti's Devastatin Duke (by Ch. Silti's Joy Boy out of Silti Tiger Rose of Tralle), bred and owned by Mary T. Estrin.

Ch. Robinson's Rudy of Elmvale (by Ch. Cypress Aristo out of Elmvale Valarie), winning Best of Opposite Sex, at twelve years of age, from the Veterans Class in a large entry. Bred by Victoria Macy and owned by Margaret John Savage. *Missy*

The Brace class is for two of the same breed that are as identical as possible in appearance; the judging is primarily based on this similarity. They should be trained to gait well together. Either a brace lead or two leads may be used. Their ownership must be identical.

The Team class is for four of the same breed, with the same requirements and procedure as the Brace class. The option here would be to use two brace leads or four single leads.

At Specialty shows, and occasionally at all-breed shows, Sweepstakes classes are held prior to the regular class judging. Those that place in their classes receive cash awards that are based on a percentage of the entry fees. These classes are for puppies and young dogs from six months to under eighteen months of age. The classes are judged by age groups for each sex. The classes are usually for dogs six to under nine months, nine to under twelve months, twelve to under fifteen months, and fifteen to under eighteen months. A Best in Sweepstakes title is awarded and, usually, a Best of Opposite Sex in Sweepstakes. Entries in these classes must also be entered in one of the regular classes at the show.

The majority of all-breed kennel clubs provide Obedience competition at their shows. This takes place in events called Obedience Trials, which are also held as separate events by Obedience Trial Clubs.

Additional details concerning the explanation of the Obedience classes should be carefully studied in the rule pamphlet. The following classes are called the regular classes. All regular classes require a total score of 170 including more than 50 percent of each exercise, in order to qualify.

The Novice A class is for dogs that have not won the Companion Dog (CD) title. The dog must be handled by the owner or co-owner or by a member of their immediate family.

The Novice B class is for dogs that have not won the CD title. In this class the dog may be handled by any person.

The Open A class is for dogs that have won the CD title but have not won the Companion Dog Excellent (CDX) title. The dog must be handled by the owner or a member of their immediate family.

The Open B class is for dogs that have won the CD or CDX title. A dog may continue to compete in this class after it has won the Utility Dog (UD) title. Dogs in this class may be handled by the owner or any other person.

The Utility A class is for dogs that have won the CDX title but have not won the UD title. Obedience judges or people who have owned, trained, or exhibited a dog that has earned an Obedience Trial championship may not enter or handle dogs in this class.

The Utility B class is for dogs that have won the Companion Dog Excellent or Utility Dog title. Dogs may not be entered in both Utility A and Utility B classes at any one trial.

The dog with the highest score in the previous classes is awarded Highest Scoring Dog in the regular classes. This is also referred to as going High in Trial. This award is the Obedience equivalent of the Best in Show win in Conformation competition.

The following are the nonregular classes that are not normally offered at all-breed shows but might be offered at Specialty shows. In these classes a qualifying score is not required to win ribbons.

The Graduate Novice class is for CD titlists that have not been certified by a judge to have received a qualifying score toward their CDX title prior to the closing of entries for the show. Dogs in this class may be handled by the owner or any other person.

The Brace class is for braces of dogs of the same breed that are eligible under AKC regulations and capable of performing the Novice exercises. They need not be owned by the same person but must be handled by one handler.

The Veterans class is for dogs that have an Obedience title and are eight or more years old prior to the closing of entries. The exercises are to be performed and judged as in the Novice class. Dogs entered in this class may not be entered in any regular Obedience class.

The Versatility class is for dogs that are capable of performing the Utility exercises. These dogs may be handled by any person and may be entered in another class at the same show. In this class six exercises are performed, two each from the Novice, Open, and Utility classes, except there are no Group exercises. The exercises are performed and judged as they are in the regular classes.

The Team class is for any four dogs that are eligible under AKC regulations. Five dogs may be entered, one to be considered an alternate for which no entry fee is required. However, the same four dogs must perform all exercises. The team does not have to be owner handled and does not have to be entered in another class. The dogs are not required to have Obedience titles.

Entry in AKC shows is not limited to dogs. People can also be entered. Young people! Most all-breed and specialty clubs offer Junior Showmanship classes at their shows.

Thirteen-year-old Christy Huff is shown winning Best Junior Handler at the 1986 Silky Terrier Club of America Specialty show, handling Ch. Chrisbonli's Williams' EDT (by Ch. Chrisbonli's Professor Silk out of Chrisbonli's Risky Business), owned by her parents, Paula and Girdley Huff. She handled the dog to major points at four shows.   *Booth*

These classes provide the opportunity for young people to compete with others in their own age group. Judging of the classes is based solely on their handling proficiency, not on the quality of their dogs.

The dog that is handled in a regular Junior Showmanship class must be entered in one of the breed or Obedience classes at the show or for Junior Showmanship only. The dog must be owned by the handler or a member of the junior's immediate family.

The American Kennel Club's booklet, *Junior Showmanship Regulations: Judging Guidelines and Guidelines for Juniors,* is available on request and should be studied for detailed information on the classes and additional rules.

The Novice class is for boys and girls who are at least ten years old and under eighteen years old. They cannot have won three first-place awards with competition.

The Open class is for boys and girls in the same age group who have won three first-place awards in the Novice class with competition.

Either or both of the above classes may be divided by age into Junior and Senior classes. The Junior class would be for those who are at least ten years of age and under fourteen years. The Senior class would be for those at least fourteen years old and under eighteen years.

The undefeated winners of these classes compete for the highly prized Best Junior Handler in Show award.

JAN

1991